# The Green-Market System

## References for the data:

References for the data can be verified by conducting an online search using the keywords mentioned in the text, enabling easy fact-checking. For further inquiries, the author can be contacted through the website findtheflaw.com.

## Acknowledgments:

This English translation was made possible thanks to the thoughtful editing of Margaret Strubel.

# The Green-Market System

# A Second Currency
# for a Parallel Economy

Essay

Vincent Lannoye

In memory of my mother.

# Table of Contents

# Alphabetical Index

# Introduction

Innovative financial tools and alternative currencies have the power to revitalize economies facing long-standing challenges. Drawing on historical examples, this book highlights how unconventional monetary approaches have influenced mainstream economies.

These innovations have offered valuable solutions during times when traditional economic thinking fell short—whether during the repeated financial crises of the 1800s, the Great Depression after 1929, or the economic stagnation of the 1970s.

Building on these precedents, the final chapter introduces a new proposal: the *Green-Market System*, featuring a parallel currency designed to reduce inequality and support the fight against global warming. Could this bold approach offer a real path forward?

*This book features selected chapters from "The History of Money for Understanding Economics," focusing on parallel currencies—monetary systems that operated alongside official currencies.*

*To provide context, each chapter begins with a brief overview of the monetary system relevant to that historical period, offering the background needed to follow the discussion.*

*For readers interested in a more comprehensive exploration of monetary systems, including their origins in early civilization, the full original work is referenced in the accompanying image.*

# The Green-Market System

# A Second Currency
for a Parallel Economy

(From past parallel currencies
to a separate green economy)

# CHAPTER 1:

# FROM THE NEW PARALLEL CURRENCY

# OF THE BANKNOTES

# TO THE INDUSTRIAL REVOLUTION

(A short introduction to monetary creation
of a parallel currency)

*Until the 17th century, the monetary system was based on a limited supply of coins. The poor often had difficulty obtaining them, while the wealthy tended to hold onto their money. Interestingly, this imbalance may not have been due solely to social inequality, but also to a basic shortage of coins.*

*• Gold and silver coins were the primary forms of currency, with 1 ounce of gold worth about 15 ounces of silver through the legal "bimetallic ratio" guaranteed by the Royal Mint. It was hardly possible to multiply coins by debasing their precious content, as people could verify it with several techniques in use since the middle ages; people were quick to reject debased coins or to move their trade to a neighboring country with better coins.*

*• Small denomination copper coinage, called "token coins," was supplemental to precious coins. Token coins were valueless metal discs struck with a recognizable seal. They were accepted in payment because they were convertible as a fractional equivalent of gold or silver coins at the Royal Mint. Token coins were always struck in limited quantities to guarantee conversions into gold or silver coins.*

*• "**Bills of exchange**" worked like certified payment slips for merchants, which could be exchanged for coins within three months. They let merchants safely store their coins in a bank and use the bills to pay others instead of carrying cash. These bills were mainly used within merchant networks and not in everyday transactions.*

*The amount of money was thus contingent on unpredictable mining, frequently causing coin shortages that significantly disrupted economic transactions. Only those who possessed coins could pay cash. Consequently, the scarcity of buyers led to a general decline in prices, a measurable phenomenon economists refer to as "deflation." This deflation was a clear indicator of economic struggles, as people were unable to sell or buy due to the lack of coins, despite the availability of goods. It was an untenable situation that necessitated change.*

# The Emergence of Banknotes to Alleviate the Money Shortage in the 17th century

## *Deflation caused by coin shortage*

From 1650 and 1730, Europe experienced economic stagnation following the earlier expansion driven by the influx of gold and silver from the Americas after 1500. This slowdown affected much of the continent, with only a few regions seeing limited growth. The downturn was primarily caused by monetary issues, rather than political ones.

The influx of gold and silver from Bohemia proved insufficient to counteract the reduced circulation of coins. Unlike the 16th century, when the production of precious metals stimulated economic activity, the diminished output no longer served as a catalyst for growth.

This situation was exacerbated by the redirection of gold and silver to India and China. After being cut off by the Turks since 1453, the resumed trade for silk and spices via routes around Africa required transactions in precious metals due to the limited appeal of European products in Asian markets.

As a result, fewer coins remained in Europe, limiting the ability to trade and carry out everyday transactions. This scarcity led to falling prices or *"deflation,"* reflecting the economic struggles of the time. Historical price data confirms that deflation occurred from 1650 until 1730.

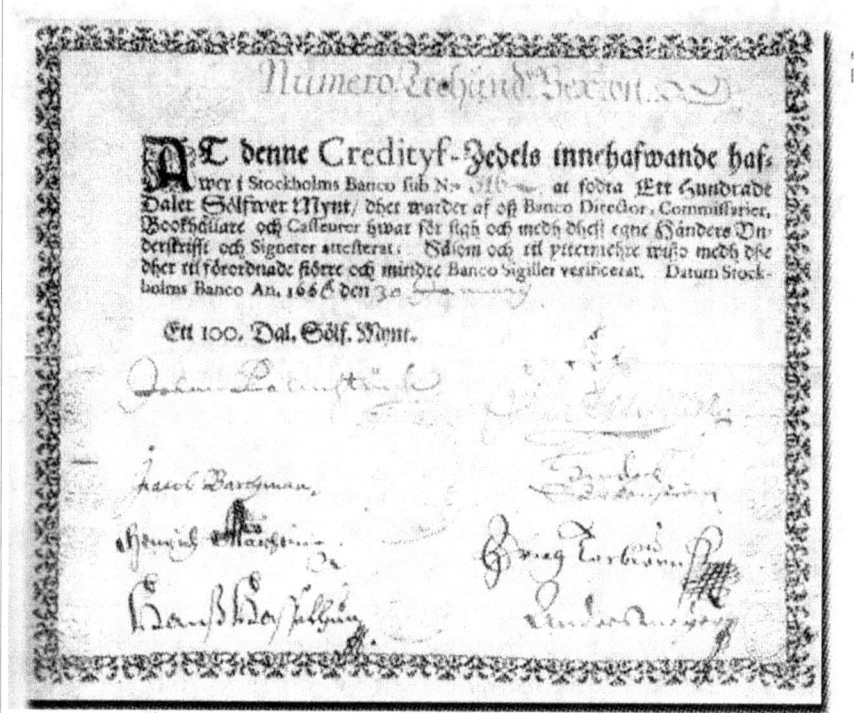

*In the late 17th century, a growing shortage of coins created a pressing need for a new form of money. This paved the way for the introduction of banknotes to circulate alongside coins. This innovation came from the private banking sector. Early banknotes worked much like bills of exchange or certified checks, promising payment in coins. Unlike checks, they did not require the signature of a potentially unverified account holder—only the signature of the renowned banker, which served as the note's guarantee.*

*The first known attempt took place in Sweden in 1666 (as shown in the image). It failed when the banker could not fulfill the promise to exchange the notes for coins, ultimately leading to the bank's bankruptcy. A few years later, banknotes began to take hold in Great Britain. There, they became an accepted part of the financial system, laying the foundation for broader economic developments that would help spark the Industrial Revolution in the 18th century.*

## Economic struggles worsened by poor politics

Economically, the prevailing governmental policy of "**mercantilism**" was detrimental to trade and production. This misguided set of policies enforced protectionism and monopolies, with the intent to preserve the circulation of the scarce gold and silver coins inside the national borders. This strategy primarily benefited established factories and industries, at the expense of any competition. While merchants and large producers grew wealthier, the majority of the population continued to struggle with poverty.

The economy was also disrupted by persistent power struggles and widespread violence, with Catholic monarchs resisting the uprisings sparked by the Renaissance and the Reformation. Moreover, European states were embroiled in numerous conflicts as they sought to complete their nation-building processes and establish regional dominance.

The stagnation was further exacerbated by the decline of Spain as Europe's leading economy. The country's wealth, heavily reliant on its American gold and silver mines, was dwindling. A significant reduction in the importation of precious metals, particularly following the decline in silver extraction from the Americas after 1650, heightened economic tensions. Moreover, this wealth drew the attention of smugglers, pirates, and privateers, leading to substantial losses. Spain's economic downturn disrupted international trade, further destabilizing the economy during this period.

*Despite a bloody civil war, the once-peripheral island of Great Britain was to restore its Saint Edward's Crown for James II (as shown in the image) and began a surprising journey toward becoming a global power.*

*This remarkable rise was driven by many factors, including a tradition of political freedom, the strength of the Royal Navy, and importantly, innovations in the financial and monetary systems.*

*History often shows that even in times of financial and political unrest, solutions can emerge through changes in the monetary system. For this reason, monetary history should not be studied in isolation, but as an integral part of both economic and political history.*

## *The rise of English banks*

Amidst a period marked by coin scarcity and deflation, the demand for borrowing surged across Europe, presenting an opportunity for organized lending operations. England distinguished itself as a hotbed for innovative financial solutions during this time. The inception of London banking can be traced back to around 1640 when King Charles I made a public attempt to confiscate gold deposits stored in the Tower of London. This move prompted anxious merchants to transfer their deposits to the goldsmith-moneychangers of London. The onset of the civil war in 1642 further accelerated this trend, with goldsmith-moneychangers receiving deposits of jewels and coins from their regular clients. These deposits transformed goldsmith-money-changers into "*bankers*," who began offering loan possibilities in coins using others' money. At the end of the civil war in 1651, the financial landscape was primed for innovative banking practices designed to expand loan capabilities in a deflationary context.

## *Interests on deposits*

London bankers recognized the central role of deposits in enabling future lending and therefore developed measures to attract depositors. They introduced various practices specifically designed to encourage deposits with the aim of expanding their lending activities.

First, to ensure depositors of the security of their assets, bankers guaranteed the safety of coins within highly secure vaults. This safe-keeping service was offered at a minimal cost, benefiting from economies of scale as the vault's security infrastructure was shared among all customers. Detailed records of each customer's deposits and withdrawals were meticulously maintained, with each customer's ledger entry being denoted as a "*bank account.*"

Second, bankers would issue nominative receipts to depositors as an attestation of their coins left in the safe. For security reasons, depositors were reluctant to carry physical coins. To cater to this, banks actively encouraged depositors to endorse their receipts as payments to other customers of the same bank. Each transaction would be diligently logged in the bank's ledger for both customers' bank accounts involved in the transaction, and remarkably, without any coin leaving the bank's vault.

Third, banks would provide bills of exchange for payments outside the purview of the bank, possibly extending to foreign countries for banks with overseas branches. These bills of exchange would be redeemed in coins at the bank's branch, but only after the standard 3-month term stipulated on the bills. In the interim, similar to the aforementioned nominal receipts, these bills could be endorsed for making payments. This practice was not novel, merely emulating the Italian and Dutch paper systems that dated back to the Renaissance.

Finally, after 1660, London banks began offering interest on deposits to attract more funds. The interest paid on deposits was financed by the interest received from loans, covering administrative and vault costs while also generating profits. This practice not only incentivized additional deposits but also underpinned the financial model that allowed London banks to flourish.

## Loans restricted to merchants and governmental entities

These deposit-oriented strategies increased coin volumes within the banks' vaults, providing an enhanced foundation for loan issuance and potential interest earnings. Loans could carefully be granted, with the coin accounting recorded by the banks for each loan account until the reimbursement of the last coin of the principal plus interest, as per the terms stipulated in the loan agreement signed by the borrower.

Undoubtedly, the primary clientele for loan services were affluent merchants and the government, who were deemed sure to pay back their loans in coins or too powerful to decline a loan request. Loans were never granted to poor people or small workshops deemed too risky of defaulting their loans.

Overall, the volume of loans granted was much lower than the volume of deposits held. Banks maintained a large portion of deposits within their vaults to ensure liquidity and the ability to fulfill withdrawal requests. This precaution limited their capacity to extend loans, even to reputable customers deemed creditworthy, despite the ongoing demand for currency, particularly in periods of deflation.

## *Appearance of banknotes*

In the late 17th century, English banks introduced a breakthrough innovation in the form of a simplified paper receipt. Instead of issuing receipts in the name of the account holder, banks issued receipts bearing only the bank's name, marked "to the bearer." This innovation marked the birth of the modern "*banknote*," which could be exchanged for coins at the issuing bank without the need for endorsement, relying solely on the bank's name for validity. The banknote could circulate among individuals until its value was claimed in coins at the issuing bank. By 1668, banknotes were recognized as a legitimate form of payment in England, and their legal status was formally ratified in 1704, laying the groundwork for the widespread use of banknotes in the early 18th century. Initially, banking services and banknotes were oriented towards merchants, bankers, and government officials, while the general population conducted transactions mostly with coins, particularly token coins.

Banknotes were issued with denominations based on silver weight and were "*convertible*" upon demand into silver coins at the issuing bank, or into gold coins according to the prevailing bimetallic ratio. Their primary denomination was the "*pound sterling*," as merchants often kept their accounts in pounds sterling and preferred notes denominated in this unit. This was despite the fact that no actual coins existed in the form of a pound sterling (112 grams of pure silver); only fractional denominations, such as the "*shilling*," worth 1/20 of a pound, were in circulation. With banknotes, the concept of the pound sterling was materialized in physical form for the first time.

Denominations of banknotes were standardized to figures rounded to hundreds, tens, or single units of pounds sterling. This addressed the impracticality of denominations with precise but cumbersome values, such as 637 pounds sterling, and enhanced the circulation of banknotes in commercial transactions.

Silver coins were minted and denominated as shillings and their respective sub-denominations, rather than in the more cumbersome form of pounds sterling of silver. These coins were defined by a high degree of purity, known as "*sterling*" silver, consisting of 92.5% silver. The value of a shilling was set at 1/20 of a pound sterling, while a silver penny held the value of 1/12 of a shilling, making the penny the

English equivalent of Charlemagne's silver denier. Additionally, silver "sixpence" coins, valued at six pennies, and silver half-crown coins, valued at 30 pennies, were also in circulation. Lower-value token coins, such as the half-penny or "halfpence," catered to the need for smaller denominations in everyday commerce.

Finally, the primary gold coin was the "*Guinea*," minted from 8.3 grams of gold with a fineness of 91.6% (equivalent to 22 carats or 22/24 purity). The value of the Guinea varied, generally aligning with approximately 20 shillings or one sterling pound of silver, subject to adjustments based on the bimetallic ratio, which typically stood at 1:15. The nomenclature "Guinea" derives from the West African region of Guinea, reflecting the geographical source of the gold used in the coin's production at that time.

*Charles I of England, as represented on the fourpence or groat coin, harbored Catholic sympathies and was a staunch proponent of the divine right of kings. This stance led to upheaval, inciting a series of Civil Wars that spanned half a century, culminating in the establishment of the Bill of Rights. Additionally, this era marked a major shift in monetary practices, transitioning from the sole issuance of coinage by royal mints to the private production of money through the issuance of paper banknotes.*

## *Loans in banknotes mitigating the effects of deflation*

Banknotes were issued as part of loan agreements, with the understanding that these loans would be withdrawn in banknotes rather than in coins. This practice equated the crediting of funds to accounts without necessitating the physical withdrawal of coins.

These banknotes, bearing the marks and signatures of reputable banks, were readily accepted by merchants because of the trust placed in these institutions. Unlike earlier paper receipts, their acceptance no longer depended on the liquidity of an individual buyer's bank account but on the reputation of the issuing bank, dissipating concerns over the financial solvency of parties involved in transactions.

Progressively, the adoption of banknotes spread beyond the traditional network of individuals with trusted bank accounts, enabling banks to broaden their customer base. This new clientele consisted of individuals willing to accept paper banknotes and open new deposit accounts without the immediate need to convert these notes into metal coins, especially for large transactions that would otherwise require cumbersome quantities of coins. This widespread acceptance of banknotes allowed banks to increase the volume of loans they could offer, while competition among banks and their banknotes fostered an environment of lower interest rates on loans.

By the early 18th century, the volume of paper money, which included both personal receipts and banknotes, had exceeded the quantity of metal coins in circulation. The English banking system played a key role in enhancing monetary circulation without reliance on gold or silver. Through the issuance of banknotes, the banking system addressed the scarcity of precious metals, thereby alleviating deflationary pressures. Historical analyses have later confirmed that England experienced less deflation compared to other countries, underscoring the effectiveness of its innovative banking practices.

## Issues of banknotes restrained by convertibility

Banks were compelled to cap the issuance of banknotes, despite borrowers' willingness to accept ever more of them. The inherent risk was that banknotes used for payments might quickly return to the issuing bank for conversion into coins, since every account holder expected the equivalent value in coins, regardless of whether they had deposited coins or banknotes. Accordingly, lending practices were cautiously calibrated to preserve a sufficient volume of coins in reserve within the banks' vaults. This adequate level of *"required reserves"* in gold or silver enabled banks to fulfill withdrawal requests and convert banknotes into coins on demand.

Banks also had to manage withdrawals efficiently. They had to let depositors claim their coins at any time to maintain confidence, while adhering to the principle of silver- or "*gold-convertibility*" for customers presenting the banknotes they had issued. They could only gently encourage, but not compel, customers to deposit returning banknotes into new deposit accounts instead of converting them.

## *First bank runs*

Throughout history, instances of bankruptcy have been recorded since ancient times. The introduction of banknotes did not eliminate such financial failures; in fact, it introduced new complexities. The earliest known issuance of banknotes in Europe is attributed to Sweden in 1661, which slightly predated their introduction in London. The pioneering banker responsible for this innovation expanded the volume of loans, which were represented by the issuance of banknotes. However, a few years after their introduction, he found himself unable to redeem the banknotes with gold and silver coins, leading to bankruptcy. This initial venture into banknote issuance ended in failure. Interestingly, the Swedish banker might have avoided the death penalty often meted out to counterfeiters of coins, possibly because the judicial system did not classify his banknotes as counterfeit currency. Nevertheless, he spent the remainder of his life in prison, marking a cautionary tale in the early history of banknote issuance.

By 1710, only two British banks had managed to endure from the early days of banking in London. The bankruptcies of other banking institutions were due to insufficient coin reserves in their vaults, which were necessary for fulfilling depositor withdrawals or for converting banknotes that explicitly pledged to "pay to the bearer on demand" in coinage. These banks had overextended themselves by issuing an excessive volume of loans, which were withdrawn in banknotes, straining the coin reserves when these banknotes were converted. The situation was exacerbated when loans defaulted, further depleting coin reserves and inevitably leading to financial crises.

Rumors of insolvency periodically triggered "*bank runs*," with depositors hastily withdrawing coins or demanding the conversion of their banknotes into gold or silver. Originating in the 17th century, as banking became widespread, bank runs occurred recurrently, precipitating cascading failures across the banking sector and impacting even stable institutions with creditworthy clientele.

A bank was vulnerable to collapse from the moment it issued its first loan exceeding its capital, especially if that loan was withdrawn in coin, reducing the available reserves. This risk persisted even with loans issued in banknotes, since the notes represented a potential demand for coin withdrawals from the vault. Even when banknotes were redeposited after transactions, the new deposits were regarded by account holders as coin equivalents, leaving them free to trigger a bank run at any time. Ultimately, the volume of deposits invariably exceeded coin reserves as soon as the first loan was issued in banknotes, making the bank susceptible to runs, payment suspensions, and bankruptcy.

Despite these challenges and periodic crises, the issuance of banknotes continued to grow, driven by the urgent need for a medium of exchange. Banknotes facilitated transactions, adhering to the principle that accepting payment in banknotes was preferable to forgoing sales altogether.

## Banks containing bank runs with high interest rates

In case of diminishing reserves of gold and silver, banks were tasked with the dual objectives of attracting deposits and curbing loans to replenish their coin reserves. To achieve this, they had little choice but to adjust interest rates, raising them to incentivize deposits and deter borrowing. During periods of financial stress, such as bank runs, interest rates could escalate to as high as 20%.

Banks were compelled to cultivate a trustworthy reputation to attract deposits and retain high-caliber clients—a strategy essential to dispelling concerns over poor loan performance and preventing bank runs. They adopted a cautious approach to lending, systematically declining applications from clients deemed high-risk or of uncertain repayment capacity. Loan approval criteria were further tightened, with borrowers required to provide extensive guarantees—a practice that underwent numerous refinements throughout the 18th century.

*Interest rates were going UP to calm down bank panics (as in the painting from 1877: The People's Bank Shortly Before the Crash). It made sense at the time, even if this move would stir up financing trouble often with dramatic consequences. Only after the crash of 1929, would the strategy change with interest rates finally trending DOWN during financial crises, while alleviating economic downturns.*

## Loan Multiplication and the Industrial Revolution in the 18th century

### *Loans with guarantors in Scotland*

In the 18th century, Scotland experienced a more acute coin scarcity compared to other regions, with banks holding minimal coin deposits. This dearth of coin reserves constrained the banks' ability to extend loans, leading to a situation where only wealthy individuals with assured repayment capabilities and assets for collateral could access loans. Such restrictive lending practices prompted a reassessment of the Scottish banking system.

Around 1730, Scottish banks adapted to this challenge by leveraging the growing acceptance of paper banknotes. They introduced innovative lending policies, such as charging interest only on the portion of a loan actually drawn, rather than on the full amount. This encouraged borrowers to withdraw only what was immediately necessary, reducing the circulation of banknotes and strengthening banks' coin reserves relative to the notes in circulation.

Scottish banks introduced another lending rule that granted loans to individuals without personal funds if those loans were backed by two guarantors. Each guarantor had to present credible financial standing as assessed by the bank. The bank could distribute the risk of unpaid loans among the borrower and his guarantors. This system leveraged strong reciprocal business relationships, enabling customers and suppliers to support each other by acting as guarantors for loan agreements. It eventually facilitated the production and delivery of goods to customers.

Upon loan approval, bank clients could utilize banknotes for their transactions, completing sales between customers and sellers using these issued banknotes. These banknotes could fund various phases of the supply chain, including the procurement of components, manufacturing wages, delivery costs, or sales delays until the final purchase. This mechanism enabled commerce even in the absence of precious coins, allowing borrowers to acquire necessary materials for production, sales, and ultimately, debt repayment. In a virtuous cycle, successful businesses would extend sponsorship to additional customers or suppliers, enabling payments in banknotes. These banknotes were used to repay the initial loan with interest, effectively circumventing the shortage of precious coins.

## Wealth without silver or gold coins

This novel banking approach drew new customers to the banks, thereby boosting their revenue through the interest accrued on meticulously approved loans. Although these interest payments were commonly made in banknotes, the widespread acceptance of this currency benefited bankers, who could employ it almost everywhere. Essentially, this meant that the banker, alongside the borrower and purchaser, realized an increase in wealth not through gold or silver coins but via goods exchanged using banknotes. The system did not increase the quantity of silver or gold in circulation, but it facilitated the production of actual goods. This framework emphasized that genuine wealth originates from productive labor and the circulation of commodities, challenging the traditional dependence on precious metal coins as the fundamental measure of wealth.

## The Industrial Revolution financed by banking and capitalism

In an unprecedented move during the 18th century, the guarantor-backed loan system broadened banking access to individuals distinguished by their technical expertise, rather than by financial assets. This innovation gave skilled Scots access to bank loans that had traditionally been reserved for merchants and governmental entities. The model quickly found favor in neighboring England, sparking a proliferation of loans in banknotes. This influx of paper money increased the capital available to corporations, thereby strengthening the foundations of capitalism. These financial resources were instrumental in transforming small-scale workshops into larger factories, supported by British banking and private investors eager to back innovative ventures. The enhanced capacity to finance the acquisition of machinery, the construction of facilities, and the payment of labor propelled the expansion of projects. Although perhaps not the initial intention, this shift had a considerable effect on the economy, representing a land-mark moment in the progression of industrial and financial practices within Great Britain.

In the 17th century, Europe had witnessed the emergence of groundbreaking technologies, propelled by the advent of the patent system, which protected and incentivized inventions. By the 18th century, the stage was set for impressive advancements both in quantity and quality across the spheres of industry and agriculture. A key milestone of this era was the development of the steam engine, which harnessed steam power to drive a variety of machinery including pumps, mills, and textile equipment. This innovation led to a cascade of further technological advancements that boosted productivity. The impact of industrial progress was felt in agriculture as well, with the introduction of stronger steel enabling the creation of more efficient plowing and harvesting tools, such as deeper plowshares and longer scythes, which replaced the traditional short sickles. Throughout the 18th century, these technological advancements increased productivity among peasants and craftsmen, enabling them to trade their enhanced outputs reciprocally. This period represented a remarkable transforma-tion in the economic landscape, laying the groundwork for the modern industrialized world.

Lastly, in the 18th century, the ascent of liberalism impacted deci-sion-making processes. Championing the principles of liberty and equal rights, liberalism was intricately connected to the emergence of the parliamentary system, stemming from the enactment of the "Bill of Rights" in 1689 during a period marked by the flourishing of Empiri-cism and the Enlightenment. This ideological wave ushered in a new era of political liberalism, which in turn laid the groundwork for economic liberalism that challenged the prevailing mercantilist doctrines of the Renaissance. The adoption of a "laissez-faire" approach within economic liberalism fostered an environment where free market competition began to erode mercantilist practices, signaling a new era in the economic and political landscape.

The confluence of financial innovation and technological ingenuity, catalyzed by the principles of liberalism, culminated in the Industrial Revolution, which commenced in Scotland and England around 1750. The ignition of the Industrial Revolution can be attributed to a myriad of factors, among which monetary and banking advancements played a central role. Indeed, the lack of sophisticated financial instruments and systems can account for the industrial stagnation observed across the European continent, despite possessing comparable technological expertise and an emerging liberal ideology. It was not until the 19th century that the European continent began to experience its own Industrial Revolution, largely due to the adoption of the British financial paradigm.

The benefits derived from the Industrial Revolution have been widely debated. It is clear that Great Britain experienced an appreciable rise in national income during this period, but it had to be shared by a population that grew by 80% in the 18th century. This demographic expansion stemmed from improved hygiene, the advent of smallpox inoculation, and greater food security driven by agricultural innovations such as crop rotation, along with the broader effects of the Industrial Revolution on agriculture and food production. However, the rapid population growth resulting from these advances disproportionately swelled the ranks of the industrial proletariat—a sector that did not equitably share in the wealth generated by the Industrial Revolution.

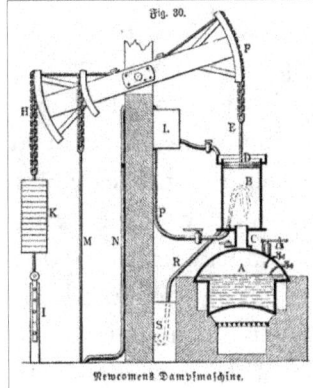

During the 18th century, the Industrial Revolution was propelled by innovations such as the Newcomen engine. Britain uniquely capitalized on this era of technological advancement by leveraging paper money or financial instruments, to fund these developments. In contrast, the European continent, constrained by its outdated financial and monetary systems, struggled to match Britain's pace of progress despite having access to coal resources and innovative ideas.

## Multiplication of paper money without inflation

In 18th century Britain, the multiplication of loans and banknotes expanded the money supply within the economy. Was there a risk of too many buyers with their hands full of too much money in the form of numerous banknotes? Too many buyers could empty too few stocks in the shops, which was pressuring shopkeepers to raise their prices and preserve some stocks for their best customers.

Prices didn't climb, as no one observed the phenomenon of general price rise, which became known as "*inflation*" by economists. Inflation is the rise of all prices, and not just of one single price. It happens when too many currency units circulate in the hands of buyers, compared to too few goods available in shops. Shopkeepers are then raising their prices as their stocks dwindle, as much as they realize that providers raise their prices as well. It is not considered as price gouging, but to sustain oneself when all prices of food and shelter are continuously rising.

This inflation would have derailed the entire system. Initially, inflation could have been compensated by a higher pay, but inflation would have definitely crushed the savings in monetary units as they were losing value compared to the prices of goods. Eventually, inflation would have struck back and depressed the economy when people decline work to save currency units soon valueless and when corporations can't sell to disgruntled workers and savers. Inflation would have started a vicious circle, as the more it climbs, the less people want to work, the less goods there are, and the more inflation feeds on itself.

Inflation didn't happen, because a counterpart in goods accompanied the increase in "*money supply*", at least as fast as the creation of money units was slowly evolving from the striking of metallic coins to the printing of paper banknotes. The main reason was that loans were granted to invest, but not to spend. Each investment was intended to produce new goods or to be more efficient in producing existing goods by saving coal, raw materials and the workforce per unit produced. The expansion of money supply via the widespread issuance of loans did not lead to inflation, except in isolated instances. Instead, profits and wages saw an uptick as production costs per unit decreased while selling prices remained constant. Thus, the proportionate increase in money units to the production of goods maintained price stability, demonstrating a balanced approach to monetary expansion and economic growth.

## Resurgence of inflation

Inflation did reappear from 1730 to 1775, but it affected the European continent as much as Great Britain. This inflation coincided with the influx of noble metals. In the 18th century, the introduction of gold was threefold that of the 16th century. The period from 1720 to 1790 saw the global gold reserves double, thanks to new finds in Brazil and the Ural Mountains of Russia. Concurrently, silver output grew due to advancements in mercury amalgamation processes, supported by consistent mercury production from mines in Spain and Slovenia. The deployment of Newcomen's steam engine for water removal from mining shafts enabled continuous, year-round mining operations.

In Europe, the inflationary phase post-1730 was characterized by a period of commercial and economic rejuvenation rather than financial instability. The influx of silver and gold adequately met the demands of an increasing population and satisfied the mercantilist desire for the hoarding of precious metals. In the end, this abundance of coins diverted European nations from adopting the British financial model.

*The Thaler of Maria Theresa, often referred to as the "dollar" of the 18th century, was a fine silver coin that garnered recognition and acceptance globally, including in the Arab world. Following the death of Empress Maria Theresa in 1780, Emperor Joseph II authorized the Austrian Mint to continue the production of this coin to meet the sustained demand emanating from the Middle East.*

*Diameter= 40mm, thickness= 2.4mm.*
*Above: Five arabesques from the edge of different thalers of post-1784 strikes (authorized to foreign Mints). These details allowed their identification. In order: Brussels, London, Paris, Vienna post-1900 and pre-1900.*

## *Money out of thin air: Scriptural money*

In the early 18th century, the adoption of paper banknotes marked a transformative moment in banking, providing an alternative to physical coinage. From then on, loans were disbursed and repaid in banknotes rather than coins. The notes circulated and were often redeposited into bank accounts without being converted back into coins. The resulting stability of coin reserves in vaults allowed banks to issue a greater volume of loans in banknote form. This evolution strengthened banks' capacity to generate interest income from lending and represented a major advancement in the mechanisms of credit and monetary circulation.

During this period, the volume of loans issued began to approach the volume of coin deposits. If a bank managed to retain a sufficient amount of coins in reserve, it could discreetly extend additional loans and generate more interest income. In practice, this meant that a bank could lend out a deposited coin more than once, creating an additional unit of currency that existed only within the bank's accounting system. This process marked the inception of "*scriptural money*," a unique form of money distinct from the official coins produced by the Mint. Through the entries in client accounts and the issuance of paper banknotes, banks were able to create scriptural money, representing a form of parallel monetary creation conducted by private entities outside the purview of the Royal Mint.

The exact date in the early 18th century when the volume of issued loans first surpassed that of deposits is uncertain. The scarcity of historical banking records prevents pinpointing the initial emergence of scriptural money. Yet this development still represented a milestone in the history of money, despite its modest impact at the time. It marked the first occurrence of parallel currency creation by private entities operating independently from official minting authorities—an innovation poised for momentous growth, with profound implications for the future of financial systems.

## Scriptural money exceeds coinage

In the late 18th century, London's financial landscape reached a remarkable level of maturity. In 1776, Adam Smith made observations that were later corroborated by historians: the volume of loans extended by banks surpassed the amount of gold and silver coins held in deposits. This marked the first sign of scriptural money. In the following decades, the scale of scriptural money created by these financial institutions reached parity with the quantity of coins officially minted. Initially, for every coin deposited, a corresponding banknote was issued, mitigating deflationary pressures. Subsequently, banks often issued a second banknote, representing purely scriptural money.

This period marked a milestone in history, when the creation of money was no longer solely a governmental prerogative exercised through minting but also extended to private banking. The issuance of banknotes and the creation of scriptural money by banks and their clients symbolized a profound shift in power dynamics, heralding a true revolution. Private banks now possessed the unprecedented ability to create money—achieving the metaphorical equivalent of the alchemists' dream of transforming lead into gold. They could allocate funds at their discretion to a wide range of beneficiaries, including nobility, commoners, merchants, engineers, and media outlets, regardless of their stance toward the Crown. This capability proved essential in financing the Industrial Revolution.

## The Bank of England and its Banknotes in the 18th century

### *The Bank of England created to fund the government*

At the end of the 17th century, amidst escalating hostilities with Louis XIV's France, the English government sought innovative financial solutions to underwrite the war effort. Confronted with wartime expenses that far exceeded tax revenues and encountering difficulties in selling bonds—partly due to the financial crisis of 1672 under King Charles II, where the King's failure to repay loans had eroded trust—the English government innovated by establishing the "*Bank of England*" ("*BoE*") in 1694. This institution was conceived with the express purpose of bolstering governmental finances, thus bypassing the challenges inherent in bond sales.

The BoE was conceived as a semi-private bank, emulating the successful model of the Bank of Amsterdam. It functioned similarly to other banks of the time, equipped with a vault, counters, discount services, and the capability to manage loans and deposits. Structured as a corporation, the BoE made its shares publicly available, and thus remaining non-refundable as long as the bank continued operations. Shareholders in need of liquidity had the option to sell their shares on the London Stock Exchange, with the selling price reflecting the anticipated dividends per share.

This institution had introduced a novel financing mechanism to the government: a perpetual loan. Essentially, the BoE leveraged its initial capital, raised through public subscriptions to its shares, to extend a perpetual loan to the Treasury in the form of coins. This arrangement of a perpetual loan alleviated the financial burden on the people by eliminating the need for heavy taxation to repay the loan's principal. Instead, the Treasury was obligated to cover only the interest payments, which were financed through the imposition of new taxes on boat tonnage and alcohol. In this sense, the establishment of the BoE marked a seminal moment in the evolution of public finance, transforming the framework of financial support available to government operations.

The capital for establishing the Bank of England was raised through the public sale of shares in exchange for coin payments. Notably, King William and Queen Mary, along with numerous private individuals, participated in the subscription, reflecting broad support and confidence in the venture. The success of the subscription surpassed expectations, largely due to the BoE's unique relationship with the government, which provided an additional layer of reassurance to investors. Additionally, the period was characterized by a speculative fervor, with investors eagerly purchasing shares in private corporations, underscoring the perceived profitability of banking ventures despite their inherent risks. In this speculative environment, the BoE, despite its governmental affiliations, was viewed as another corporation with promising investment potential.

## *The popular banknotes of the BoE*

The BoE engaged in traditional banking activities, accepting coin deposits and granting loans, which were issued in its own banknotes. These notes were convertible into coins at the bank's counters. Despite its status, the BoE was not immune to the risks that afflict private banks, including the threat of a bank run. In 1696, for example, the bank faced a crisis precipitated by individuals who viewed it as unjust competition to private banking interests. These critics, aiming to undermine the BoE, spread rumors about a shortage of coin reserves in an effort to destabilize the institution. Their tactics included orchestrating mass withdrawals of coins, which led to a sharp decline in the bank's stock value amid investor panic. Ultimately, the BoE withstood this concerted effort to compromise its stability.

In response to these challenges, several measures were implemented to fortify the BoE and to enhance the security and reliability of its banknotes. First, counterfeiting the BoE's banknotes was made punishable by death, aligning with the existing penalties for falsifying Royal Mint coins. Second, starting from 1722, the BoE began to amass a gold reserve to strengthen its solvency and ensure the convertibility of its notes. Third, the BoE was granted a monopoly on the issuance of banknotes, although this was effectively bypassed by private banks.

Over time, the BoE's banknotes gained unprecedented popularity. Clients progressively consented to receive these notes instead of gold coins for withdrawals from their accounts at private banking institutions. Consequently, most private banks established loan accounts with the BoE, using its banknotes as part of their reserves for managing deposit withdrawals and for the conversion of their own banknotes. Within a few decades, the practice of converting private banknotes into gold coins shifted towards conversion into BoE banknotes. For private banks, reserves in pounds sterling, earmarked for covering deposit withdrawals and the exchange of banknotes, were increasingly denominated in BoE notes alongside traditional gold and silver coins.

Customers progressively chose to withdraw their loans in BoE banknotes rather than those issued by private banks, leading to a decline in the issuance of private banknotes. However, it wasn't until 1844 that the BoE was formally granted the exclusive right to issue banknotes, with exceptions allowed for banks that had been established prior to this legislation. Following this enactment, the number of private banks authorized to issue their own notes gradually diminished. The last license permitting an English private bank to issue its own banknotes was revoked following a bank merger in 1921, signaling the end of an era for private banknote issuance.

*Sir Isaac Newton is celebrated on a modern banknote by the Bank of England, acknowledging not only his monumental contributions to science but also his involvement in monetary regulation, evidenced by his 27-year tenure as Master of the Mint. This period of service underscores the breadth of his intellect and curiosity, which extended well beyond the confines of any single discipline.*

## BoE under supervision

The Bank of England steadfastly maintained the convertibility of its banknotes into gold or silver. This policy subjected the issuance of banknotes to public scrutiny through prompt gold conversion but was limited by the BoE's sole location in London. In reality, the English monetary system operated as a tiered system: private banknotes were convertible into BoE banknotes, which, in turn, could be exchanged for gold coins within the capital. This pyramidal structure helped alleviate deflation caused by coin shortages.

In addition, the Bank of England could not loan its convertible banknotes to the Treasury without parliamentary approval. The BoE repeatedly affirmed its commitment to limiting such financial assistance to the Treasury. This assurance was occasionally overlooked, causing tension in Parliament over these practices.

## Regulations on private banknotes

In the 18th century, regulatory measures were implemented to curb the excessive issuance of banknotes by private banks, which were leveraging swift profits from easy bank loans. To mitigate the risks associated with the over-issuance of low-denomination banknotes—seldom presented for coin conversion—minimum denominations were established. In Scotland, banknotes were required to have a minimum denomination of one pound, while in England, the BoE banknotes were subject to a minimum of five pounds. Private banks in England, however, retained the liberty to issue banknotes of any denomination.

Furthermore, the inclusion of the phrase "pay to the bearer on demand" on banknotes was mandated, eliminating delayed conversion with phrases such as "pay to the bearer in a few months." This measure addressed the over-issuing of banknotes to support risky loans by ensuring immediate convertibility. Aside from these regulations, most other banking practices remained permissible and were at times even legally endorsed for use in payments and contractual agreements.

## The BoE stabilizing private banks

The BoE assumed the role of lender of last resort for private banks facing insolvency. These BoE emergency loans, issued in its banknotes under specific conditions, could alleviate the concerns of clients associated with banks at risk of failure. Such assistance was conditional: the BoE had to retain sufficient gold reserves in its vaults; it required precise and transparent accounting from prospective borrowers, including distressed private banks; and it scrutinized their integrity and honesty before assuming the responsibility of maintaining stability in the banking sector.

This stabilization effort gave the government a mandate to regulate private banks, especially after the destabilizing speculative "South Sea Bubble" of 1720, when South Sea Company stock soared to unsustainable heights before collapsing, causing widespread financial ruin and a severe economic downturn. From then on, new banking institutions were subject to stringent conditions not applied to their predecessors, most notably a restriction to six shareholders. The regulation aimed to prevent a recurrence of such a crisis by limiting collective losses to only a few shareholders of a single entity. However, this shortsighted restriction also hampered new banks' ability to raise capital through share issuance, constraining their operations. The shareholder limit was not relaxed until 1826 for banks near London and was finally repealed nationwide in 1865. This law played a significant role in stifling monetary creation and contributed to Britain losing its industrial edge throughout the 19th century. This regulatory misstep was far from being the last in the realm of banking regulations.

# Historical Correlation: The Industrial Revolution Beyond Government Interference

Historical research has delved into the role of banking institutions in generating money supply, revealing their contribution to financing the Industrial Revolution. This watershed period was intrinsically linked to the preceding Financial Revolution in Great Britain, suggesting that the industrial advancements of the era could not have occurred in the absence of banks.

This Financial Revolution was sparked by private individuals who introduced original banknotes and loans with guarantors outside of the Royal monetary system. This groundbreaking parallel financing allowed individuals to escape the constrained loop of precious coins flirting with deflation, and to provide the means to inventors and technicians to create new machines and transition from manual labor to the scalable techniques of the Industrial Revolution.

Wisely, the British government refrained from interfering at the time of the Industrial Revolution. It let the money supply shift from the coin striking of its Royal Mint to the creation of banknotes and scriptural money through the bank accounts of private individuals. The British government could then extend its economic hegemony over the world, hoisting the Union Jack on five continents.

In contrast, other nations have struggled to contest the economic dominance of Great Britain. These nations only jumped on the train of the Industrial Revolution several decades after Great Britain, and not without experiencing a few notable self-inflicted setbacks along the way.

*The Industrial Revolution served more as a milestone of progress rather than regression. Nations experienced increased wealth, albeit with an unequal distribution of benefits. Notably, the lives of women saw considerable improvements over the pre-industrial era, which was dominated by labor-intensive activities such as fieldwork, high fertility rates, and elevated risks of mortality during childbirth. The shift to a lifestyle supported by mass-produced medicine and improved provisioning was a major breakthrough. However, its initial impact was offset by population growth, as more children survived. Only later did it begin to contribute significantly to reducing poverty. A return to pre-industrial conditions would pose challenges, arguably sustainable only for men in perfect health.*

# CHAPTER 2:

# PARALLEL CURRENCIES:

# HICCUPS OF THE 18TH CENTURY

(When governments messed up
monetary creation)

*Deflation was a recurrent issue since the Middle Ages, as the lack of coins in circulation impeded transactions, taxation, and even charitable donations. To circumvent this monetary trap, various strategies were employed to keep the economy functioning despite the constraints of deflation. One such example was the creation of charity tokens not convertible into gold or silver (Picture: charity token of Saint Martin parish in Liège, Belgium). These tokens circulated locally and were often modified to prevent counterfeiting. They were distributed to the poor for attending Sunday mass and could later be spent at bakeries but not at beer taverns. Eventually, bakers could exchange these tokens for regular coins.*

*Throughout the 18ᵗʰ century, other monetary experiments with parallel currencies were attempted to avoid deflation, stimulate the economy, and even emulate Great Britain. These experiments were not always successful, often failing due to government interference.*

# Banknotes Discredited in France After 1720

## *The Régent influenced by John Law*

Following the death of King Louis XIV of France in 1715, an era ended, leaving France politically and religiously unified but financially strapped. The nation's involvement in countless wars with Protestant neighbors had drained the royal treasury. Additionally, the French government faced challenges in securing further loans from domestic banks, which were constrained by the scarcity of coin deposits. During this period, coins represented the sole medium of exchange, necessitating their preservation by the people for transactional purposes. The French banking system was lagging behind British developments.

In this context, Régent Philippe d'Orléans, who governed pending the majority of Louis XV, paid heed to John Law, a recent immigrant from Scotland. Law, having experienced rejection from the Scottish Parliament for his innovative banknote issuance proposal backed by real estate instead of gold, found a receptive audience in the Régent. Law's advocacy for utilizing loans and paper currency to combat unemployment during a period of widespread deflation across Europe was visionary. He argued convincingly that a robust economy required liquidity to facilitate trade, which in turn, would generate revenue through taxation for the treasury.

In response, in 1716, the Régent granted John Law the authority to establish a pioneering bank with the sole right to issue banknotes in the Paris region. These notes were convertible into precious metals—silver or gold—abandoning the real estate backing that Law had originally envisioned. This convertibility was guaranteed by the value of the precious coins constituting the bank's capital, which was supported by Law's personal investment and that of other stakeholders. The bank issued notes in denominations of 10, 50, and 100 French pounds, or "livres tournois," which was the standard monetary unit for both accounting and coinage purposes.

The bank could start its various financial operations. Of particular importance was the "*discounting*" of bills of exchange. This service involved the bank extending a cash advance against these bills, prior to the stipulated payment deadline mentioned on them, in return for a "discount fee". Unlike traditional methods that utilized coins, these cash advances were provided in the form of banknotes, a measure designed to bolster the utility and circulation of paper money.

## The system of John Law

Endowed with the exclusive authority to issue banknotes, John Law sought to enhance their attractiveness and discourage their rapid conversion back into coins.

Law managed to centralize the collection of all public revenues through the bank. He required tax collectors to accept banknotes as payment, specifically targeting Treasury creditors involved in tax farming, allowing them to repay their loans to the government with banknotes. He also mandated that all taxes beyond those collected by tax farmers be remitted to Paris exclusively in Law's banknotes. This regulation increased the circulation of banknotes because of the geographical distance between the provinces and Paris, while also alleviating cash scarcity in the provinces by eliminating the need to transport coins physically to the capital.

Recognizing the untapped potential of France's vast territories in North America, Law founded the Company of the West ("Compagnie d'Occident") in 1717. This entity aimed to stimulate trade with Louisiana, through the acquisition of ships, and swiftly secured a monopoly over the fur trade with Canada and the entire Louisiana territory. The ambition was that the company's activities would generate a flow of coins back to France through international trade. Investment in the company was exclusively via Law's banknotes, with shares traded on the Paris stock exchange, located on Quincampoix Street. Anticipated high returns on these shares made banknotes an attractive means of investment. Many individuals responded by investing their banknotes in shares instead of exchanging them for coins, and the bank's reserves of precious metals saw a marked increase.

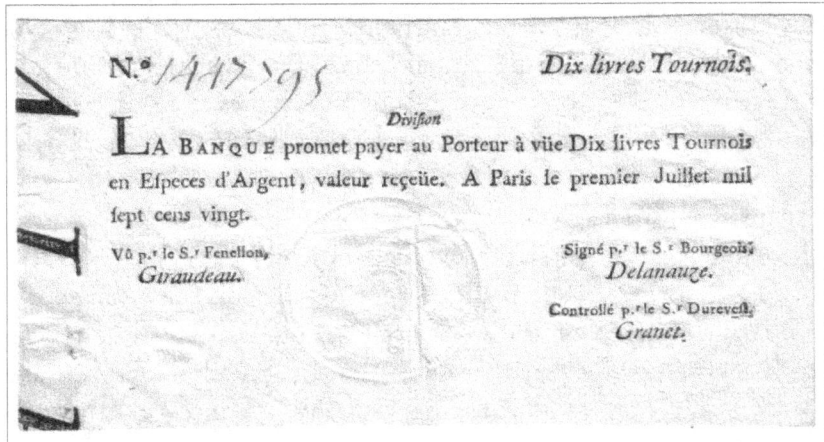

*Banknotes issued by John Law's bank were recognized as valid currency for purchasing shares, whose value escalated remarkably from 500 to 18,000 pounds. The French people were experiencing the frenzy of speculation within the stock market for the first time.*

## Chaotic issues of banknotes and speculation in shares

In 1718, the French government consolidated control over John Law's bank by acquiring shares from Law and other stakeholders, converting it into a royal institution. This transition placed the operations of crediting, issuing, and printing banknotes under the directives of the Council of State. Despite Law's warnings, the Council succumbed to the allure of expanding the paper currency supply to finance governmental expenses.

Banknotes were initially embraced by the public, associated as they were with ownership in the Company of the West and its promising dividends. The company enjoyed a prosperous phase, bolstered by its fleet, monopolies, and positive early outcomes. The circulation of banknotes increased across the kingdom, mirroring the surge in the company's share prices at the stock exchange. It was even reported that individuals attempted to convert their silver coins into banknotes to invest in shares, although the bank refused such exchanges.

Law lost control over the bank but continued to manage the Company of the West. In 1719, the company expanded by absorbing other trading companies dealing with India and China, despite their sizable debts transferred from the French government. This consolidation positioned Law at the helm of France's maritime trade. Moreover, the company took on the substantial debt of the French government in exchange for future tax revenues, issuing new shares to repay creditors. Thus, creditors transitioned from lenders to shareholders, exchanging potential interest payments for prospective dividends from the company's ventures, effectively transforming the national debt into a perpetual investment similar to the model used by the BoE.

By 1720, a wave of speculation propelled the company's share price to unparalleled levels on the stock exchange, indicative of the nascent French foray into stock market dynamics. In fact, this surge in value was artificially inflated due to the excessive issuance of banknotes, captivating speculative investors.

The same year marked a downturn for the company, with profits falling short of expectations and damaging rumors circulating. A noticeable discrepancy emerged between prices in banknotes and those in coins, revealing inflationary pressures exacerbated by the overabundance of paper currency. This inflation advantaged transactions in coins, offering better value, leading to a sharp and devastating correction in the market and public confidence.

## Collapse of the system

In 1720, the value of the Company's shares plummeted. This depreciation diminished the attractiveness of the banknotes issued by John Law's bank, as the public became increasingly reluctant to accept them as payment. The depreciation of share value and the ensuing disrepute of banknotes culminated in widespread financial ruin among holders. The suspension of banknote conversion into precious metals became unavoidable, leading directly to bankruptcy. As a consequence, those in possession of the banknotes faced the grim reality of their worthlessness.

The severe drop in share value and the discredit of banknotes resulted in Law being scapegoated for the financial turmoil, with the government dissociating itself from the crisis. Although the bank was under royal ownership, John Law, as the architect of this financial system, was held accountable for the fiasco. Critics persuaded the Régent to dismiss Law, resulting in the confiscation of the Company's assets and reducing it to insignificance by 1721. The collapse resonated throughout Europe, with Law bearing the brunt of the blame.

The aftermath sparked debate over whether Law's financial system was designed to alleviate government debt at the expense of the population, suggesting that the government may have intentionally defaulted. Whether Law personally profited from the system remains doubtful, particularly given his hasty departure from France and his impoverished demise.

Historians have meticulously analyzed Law's system, reaching varied conclusions about its intentions and viability. The evidence does not conclusively prove that Law's system was doomed from the outset. Removed from his position prematurely, Law did not have the opportunity to rectify the situation. His brilliance was as evident as his recklessness, and his downfall was exacerbated by unfounded rumors and the government's mishandling of the bank's administration.

*Drawing of John Law from a chocolate box with some comments on the reverse: "At the advent of the duke of Orléans as Régent, the financial business of France was in an embarrassing situation. The duke listened to Law. In 1716, Law established with the patronage of the duke a bank supported by the royal authority. He also founded the company of Mississippi with the aim of profiting from the French possessions in North America. In the fever which followed, this company's shares went up to 35 or 40 times their face value. But the decrease of profits and the continual issue of banknotes by the government, destroyed the company and Law had to flee. He was always an honest man whose purpose was only to improve people's lives..."*

## Aftermath of the failure

The aftermath of the banknote debacle left a lasting impression on the collective memory, halting the issuance of banknotes in France and perpetuating coin scarcity. This deflationary situation threatened to sideline France from the burgeoning Financial and Industrial Revolutions due to the absence of banknote-based lending. The French people risked enduring the repercussions of governmental misconduct for years. It was only with the inflow of precious metals between 1730 and 1775 that France averted a potential deflationary crisis.

In 1776, the French government took steps towards establishing a new institution with the mandate to issue banknotes, mirroring the principles of Law's Bank. This institution, named the "Caisse d'Escompte," specialized in the discounting of bills of exchange for a fee, providing payment in banknotes that were convertible into coins upon demand. The "Caisse" expanded its operations as taxes became payable in its banknotes, and tax farmers were mandated in 1778 to accept this form of payment, eventually leading to the provision of loans in banknotes. The success of the "Caisse" can also be attributed to the prevailing lack of currency and the return of deflation post-1780, exacerbated by France's continued dependence on precious metal coins—a vulnerability not shared by Great Britain with its extensive use of banknotes.

This endeavor in banknote issuance endured for a decade until the dissolution of the bank, at which point its banknotes were exchanged for another form of paper currency, the Assignats, introduced during the French Revolution. This transition and its implications are explored further in subsequent sections.

## Debacle of the "Continentals" in the US Around 1780

### *Issues of credit notes*

Throughout the 18th century, the British American colonies faced a shortage of silver and gold coins, which adversely affected their economic growth. This dearth of precious metals restricted the colonies' ability to establish private banking institutions that could issue banknotes exchangeable for silver or gold. Similarly, the scarcity impeded the formation of a public bank comparable to the Bank of England. This shortage of currency likely resulted in deflation, although historical price data on the subject is limited.

To circumvent the lack of currency, several colonies adopted the issuance of "*credit notes*" as a remedial measure. These were essentially paper acknowledgments issued by colonial authorities, signifying a nominal debt owed by the government to the note's holder. Analogous to contemporary Treasury bonds but of lower value, these credit notes were issued to finance government expenditures. They represented a promise of repayment, either in coinage or small parcels of land, over an extended period and with accrued interest. Denominations of these notes reflected the limited currencies then in circulation, primarily English pounds and Spanish dollars.

The main incentive to accept these paper notes in payment was the severe shortage of hard currency at the time. The credit notes circulated in the American colonies largely because of the scarcity of gold and silver coins. Furthermore, they were sometimes accepted because they carried a "*legal tender*" status—denoting a legal obligation to accept the currency as payment—in particular to pay taxes.

Ultimately, the prerogative of monetary creation resided with the government through the issuance of credit notes to fund its spending. This approach stood in stark contrast to the model in Great Britain, where the expansion of the money supply originated from the collaborative efforts of private individuals and banks, with the money aimed at investment purposes.

*A Continental note denominated at seven Spanish dollars, February 1776, just before the American declaration of independence.*

## *The "continentals" of the American Revolution*

In 1775, the American colonies declared their intention to self-govern, leading to the outbreak of war with England. To finance itself, the new confederal or "Continental" Congress didn't want to resort to taxation. Taxation in-kind or in coins was hated by most Americans. Taxation was the strong reason to rebel against England. For a long time, the thirteen colonies had exclaimed, "No taxation without representation" at the Houses of Parliament in London.

Left with limited options, the Continental Congress of the States of America was compelled to finance its operations through the issuance of credit notes known as "***continentals***." The acceptance of these continentals remained voluntary. The rationale for their usage as a medium of exchange was predicated on the promise that they would eventually be redeemable for coins, coupled with the accrual of interest payable in gold or silver.

*A Continental note of 60 dollars, issued in 1778, which was likely produced by British forces with the aim of exacerbating inflation. This instance represents an early example of such tactics in warfare. By early 1781, the devaluation of this paper money led to mutinies among American soldiers, despite previous victories. Only the intervention of France, under King Louis XVI, averted a crisis by providing essential support. This included a loan of silver coins to pay soldiers before the final battle at Yorktown.*

## Heading toward inflation

The Continental Congress and the individual states within the confederation increased the issuance of their respective currencies, "continentals" and "state notes," to fund their expenditures. This proliferation of paper currency quickly exceeded prudent limits, leveraging the efficiency of the printing press to bypass the constraints associated with traditional coin minting.

As a consequence, inflation surged, driven by merchants' reluctance to accept the notes at their nominal value in silver or gold. The value of both continentals and state notes rapidly depreciated, leading to astronomical inflation rates. When these currencies were accepted, it was at highly inflated and speculative rates, leading to widespread financial instability.

This shift from a state of bothersome deflation to rampant inflation resulted in mounting losses for those who had stashed these notes. By 1781, the value of continentals had plummeted to just 1/100 of their original value in silver or gold, severely impacting the livelihoods of American soldiers paid in this devalued currency and precipitating mutinies that nearly led to the collapse of the American military effort. It was only the intervention of France, with its provision of warships, troops, and crucially, silver coins, that averted disaster at Yorktown.

Nationally, the continental's value further declined to 1/1000 of its face value, leading to financial turmoil that incited riots and violence, even as the colonies achieved independence. This period underscored the volatile nature of unbacked paper currency and the economic challenges faced by the fledgling nation.

## Liquidation of the credit notes

In 1783, the issuance of Continental notes ceased with the conclusion of the war and the ratification of the Treaty of Independence. The newly established Treasury had no option but to introduce a new series of bonds sold for cash. These bonds were underpinned by a commitment to repay the interest and principal in gold or silver coins, which facilitated the sale of the bonds or their acceptance in payments. The coins stipulated on the bonds were the American dollars, constituted by gold (24.75 troy grains) or silver (371.25 troy grains), establishing a bimetallic system at a 1:15 ratio. The dollar was further divided into 100 cents, represented by token coins. From 1793, these newly minted coins replaced the Spanish dollar coins, French silver "ecus" and English sterling shillings still in circulation.

The promise to redeem the Continental notes at their nominal value in gold or silver proved unattainable. By 1791, the Continental currencies were exchanged at 1/100 of their nominal value for gold or silver, though exclusively in the form of new Federal Treasury bonds. This process also included the repurchase of state-issued notes by the federal government, with a preferential treatment for states that had managed their finances prudently. For instance, Virginia received compensation through the establishment of the new federal capital,

Washington D.C., within its borders (alongside Maryland). This arrangement concluded the Continental currency saga, marking it as the first instance of "*fiat money*" in history. Fiat money is defined as paper currency issued by a government without intrinsic value or guaranteed convertibility into precious metals.

## A new monetary system in the early United States

Under the provisions of the 1787 Constitution, the United States federal government assumed control over currency issuance. Previous ambiguities in currency issuance between individual states and the confederal authority had plunged the nation into financial disarray. This experience highlighted the need for a unified monetary policy, resulting in a consensus to centralize monetary powers at the federal level and eliminate state-level currency issuance.

In 1793, the new federal United States Mint in Philadelphia began minting new dollar coins. From 1793 onward, these coins gradually replaced the Spanish dollar coins, French silver "ecus" and English sterling shillings still in circulation.

In this emerging financial landscape, federal bonds became a crucial supplement to the limited supply of coins. Alexander Hamilton, the first Secretary of the Treasury, established a financial marketplace in New York in 1792 to enhance the liquidity and market acceptance of these bonds. This venture began under a tree on Wall Street. This development permitted the occasional conversion of bonds into precious metal coins, thereby enhancing their liquidity. It also positioned these bonds as comparable to gold or silver ingots in terms of financial utility. Such advancements were vital in bolstering the value and practicality of bonds within an economy grappling with precious metal scarcity.

Concurrently, the licensing of private banks to issue banknotes, backed by coins or possibly federal bonds, represented another major advancement. This approach placed a chunk of monetary creation in the hands of merchants, entrepreneurs, and their private banks. These entities were authorized to issue banknotes under state charters, convertible into standard dollar coins, thus expanding the monetary base beyond federal issuance.

Distinct from the British model, the United States did not establish a central banking institution akin to the Bank of England, capable of issuing and standardizing paper money nationwide. The US Constitution's ambiguity on this matter delayed the establishment of a central bank, a debate that persisted until the establishment of the Federal Reserve Bank in 1913.

*The Continental dollar coin, conceived in 1776, was initially intended to be minted from precious metals to redeem Continental paper currency, which was issued to fund the war effort. Due to a scarcity of silver, the mint resorted to using brass and tin for the coinage. This deviation from the original plan contributed to the discredit of the currency, giving rise to the phrase "Not worth a continental." Featured on the reverse side of the coin were the inscriptions "Fugio" (Latin for "Time flies") and "Mind your business," phrases attributed to Benjamin Franklin.*

## Collapse of the Assignats of the French Revolution

### Creation of the assignat in 1789

The French Revolution began in July 1789. Soon afterward, the worried upper class started hoarding their silver and gold coins, with large amounts being moved to safer foreign locations. This disappearance of coins further exacerbated the currency shortage and the inherent deflation that had been plaguing Europe, especially after 1780.

In December 1789, a substitute form of currency was introduced in response to the dwindling coin supply. The newly formed French parliament, known as the "Assemblée nationale," issued the first paper notes called "*assignats*," denominated in French pounds ("livres tournois"). The assignat functioned as a short-term micro-bond with a six-month duration (concluding in July 1790), redeemable in land and buildings that had been confiscated from the Church. The term "assignat" is derived from historical legal practices where land could be "assigned" as collateral for a loan, positioning the assignat between fiat money and banknotes. It shared characteristics with fiat money due to its initial inconvertibility, at least on demand, and with banknotes through its eventual convertibility into land within a stipulated time-frame, a concept reminiscent of schemes by John Law before 1720.

To make these quasi-Treasury bonds more appealing, a 5% interest rate was applied. However, it was the deflation, more than the interest incentive, that pressed for the assignats' widespread acceptance and circulation, along with speculative views treating them akin to shares in land. This broad acceptance included even moneychangers, who were willing to exchange a one-pound assignat for one pound in coins.

At the end of the six-month term, the initially promised land redemption for the assignats was unexpectedly rescinded, with the allocated 5% interest rate being cited as the justification for this decision. As a result, the assignats were transformed into inconvertible fiat currency.

In its initial two years, the assignat remained stable as the revolutionary authorities exercised restraint in issuing this new paper currency as an alternative to silver or gold. The French parliament printed assignats in proportion to the collateralized lands, utilizing them to cover governmental expenditures. This method of issuance and expenditure managed to compensate, quite honorably and without inciting inflation, for the coin scarcity and the dip in consumption attributed to hoarding.

Fortunately, the circulation of assignats helped alleviate the low tax revenues resulting from hastily implemented fiscal reforms. A new income-proportional tax system replaced the widely disliked royal sales tax, but the tax administration's inexperience in assessing citizens' incomes led to poor tax collection.

*Assignat of 15 "sols" (1 pound = 20 sols) printed in 1793 with the promise of payment in land at the end of a fixed term. The overprinting of these notes contributed to the economic debacle followed by the bloody "Terreur."*

## Inflation and economic crisis

In April 1792, France declared war on Austria as a preemptive measure against potential invasion and as a diversion from domestic political unrest and economic challenges. Historian François Crouzet suggests that monetary factors may have influenced the revolutionary government's aggressive posture. Specifically, the depreciation of the French pound in assignats relative to foreign currencies presented a deep concern. For the French parliament, maintaining the assignat's nominal value on the international stage served as an additional incentive to persuade King Louis XVI, who was still reigning at that time, to attack Austria and its allies. The expectation was that a swift and successful military campaign would validate the assignat's inconvertibility and enable the liquidation of nationalized properties without the constraints previously associated with the currency.

In the ensuing months, the volume of assignats swelled dramatically to finance the war efforts, leading to rampant inflation, particularly for transactions conducted in assignats. The discrepancy between the assignat's nominal value and its purchasing power in gold or silver became increasingly pronounced, giving rise to a dual pricing system. By April 1793, attempts to outlaw dual pricing merely accelerated the disappearance of metallic coins from circulation. Inflation in prices in assignats became inescapable.

This inflationary spiral caused widespread market disarray and deepened the economic crisis, characterized by uncertainty, black markets, smuggling activities, and even insurrections. The adverse economic conditions severely disrupted production across various sectors. Manufacturers, farmers, and traders were deterred from producing goods due to the diminishing value of assignats, exacerbating the disparity between the supply of goods and the amount of currency in circulation. This vicious cycle of inflation, production decline, and further inflation sharply reduced overall economic activity.

The devaluation of assignats was so acute that payments made with them were perceived as tantamount to confiscation. Various forms of resistance to accept assignats emerged, including exorbitant pricing, hoarding of supplies, and outright refusal of sale. Consumers were forced to pay with coins or face starvation. On rare occasions where assignats were accepted, it was either out of speculative intent or under coercion. The economic activity contracted to subsistence levels, drastically reducing the people's purchasing power and fueling widespread discontent and disobedience.

## *The assignats and the Terror*

Throughout 1793, the imperative to finance military operations intensified the printing of assignats, precipitating rampant inflation that fueled growing opposition to the revolutionary government. This dissent was interpreted as betrayal of the French Revolution, prompting its leaders to adopt increasingly radical measures.

In September 1793, the Revolution entered its most severe phase, known as the Reign of Terror, marked by extreme repression carried out by figures infamously called the Terrorists. This period was characterized by widespread executions, justified by the leaders as necessary actions to safeguard the Revolution.

In July 1794, the people, exhausted by the widespread executions that characterized the Terror, established a new governing body, the Directoire. Despite repelling external adversaries, the new administration struggled to implement economic reforms. The printing of assignats continued unabated leading to an inflationary peak in 1795.

By this time, the value of assignats had plummeted drastically in comparison to silver or gold denominations, contributing to a severe economic downturn and rampant inflation. This economic instability culminated in food shortages, sparking riots among the inhabitants of Paris in May 1795. In an attempt to address these issues, a nominal reform was introduced, featuring assignats denominated in "francs" of the Revolution, with one franc theoretically equivalent to 4.5 grams of silver, in alignment with the newly adopted metric system. In reality, this change was largely superficial, as the franc-denominated assignats were not actually convertible.

## Liquidation of the assignats

In February 1796, the authorities finally dismantled the printing presses for assignats. They remained in circulation for several months but were frequently rejected as a form of payment. On occasions when assignats were accepted, their value plummeted to less than 1/300 of their nominal value in silver or gold. By August 1796, the assignat was officially phased out as an authorized method for the payment of certain taxes.

In 1796, France transitioned back to a monetary system anchored in silver and gold coinage. This shift was successfully navigated despite potential risks of deflation, thanks to favorable economic developments that attracted precious metals from international sources. Furthermore, the accumulation of gold and silver, derived from the spoils of France's military victories across Europe, bolstered the national treasury. This wealth from the military also paved the way for a coup d'état led by a young general named Napoleon, ushering a new epoch in the nation's history.

# Historical Correlation: Monetary Mismanagement and Money Illusion

With currency collapses, the American and French people of the 18th century fell victim to the financial mismanagement of their respective governments dazzled by *"money illusion"*. These ill-advised governments believed that money is worth a product one day, then more money will surely be worth more products the next day. People must watch out for this money illusion.

Misled by money illusion, governments may resort to an artificial multiplication of banknotes, assuming that such a move will boost the economy. It will cultivate an illusory sense of wealth for the people receiving the banknotes, but it cannot perk up consumption for long. The revival of business with freshly printed banknotes from compulsory bank loans would only be temporary.

In the face of such financial manipulation, prices would rapidly rise and soon anticipate this inflation. Individuals would lament about the rise of prices; their savings would lose later what they believed to have gained earlier; their spending cuts would depress the economy. Worst case scenario, once inflation has surfaced, it might skid in an inflationary spiral, possibly hyperinflation, which has the potential to wreak severe havoc on the economy.

Money illusion should never deceive anyone, even less so in modern times without the excuse of the 18th century regarding inexperience with banknotes. People must remain steadfast in their core principles and beware of the easy money from demagogic governments. It is labor and output that counts, not currency units. It is workshops and corporations that produce wealth, not the national central bank or the Treasury. It is the economy and jobs that will provide for welfare and defense, not the bureaucracy. It is the people and liberty that truly matter, not the mandates of the government.

# CHAPTER 3:

# ALTERNATIVE CURRENCIES:

# ESCAPING GOVERNMENT CONTROL

(An alternative market to bypass
government regulations)

As in past centuries, alternative currencies continue to circulate in our modern society. Despite their relative obscurity, these unconventional methods of settling transactions play a role in curbing government overreach.

Gold, with its value underpinned by robust demand in the metal exchange markets, stands as one of these alternative forms of currency. It may still be utilized in transactions, contingent upon the mutual consent of all parties involved. After the transaction, gold can possibly be converted into dollars. Legally, such a transaction must be reported to the IRS at gold's fair value in dollars.

The inherent value of gold ensures its continued relevance within the monetary system, preventing a full control of the authorities over currency. Advocates for more governmental oversight have voiced the idea of phasing out physical banknotes in favor of electronic transactions through credit cards or mobile apps. This proposition is predicated on the belief that transitioning to a cashless system would enhance the ability of agencies such as the IRS and FBI to monitor financial transactions. Realistically, this suppression of banknotes would have little effect, because people and especially gangsters can always use universal gold coins for transactions under the table to buy illicit drugs, avoid taxation, and sell gold "found" in the deep sea to re-enter bank accounts in a low-tax country. With pervasive gold coins, the suppression of banknotes could have the same fate as the Prohibition of the 1920s intended to curb alcohol consumption, but only ending up boosting organized crime.

## The Black Market: A Parallel Market to Boost Low Wages

### *The black market's role in alleviating inequality*

The "*black market*" is too often ignored by economists. The black market, also called "underground economy" or "smuggling," has a primary aim being to circumvent government regulations such as bans, taxation, and customs duties. The black market has always existed in parallel to the regular economy, from antiquity to present days.

The black market should be studied for its potential to alleviate poverty. It can serve as a lifeline for disenfranchised individuals who break the law under circumstances that may be considered forgivable. The black market can indeed serve as a support system for the poorest, especially during economic crises and periods of job loss. The black market is not solely about international criminal activity, which justifies the armies of officers trying to fight it. In many countries, black market participants are often unarmed individuals and small businesses who conduct transactions in cash to avoid taxes. These participants typically operate in sectors that are difficult to regulate, such as construction, retail, and vehicle maintenance and repair. These minor offenders are frequently overlooked by law enforcement, particularly in regions of Europe and Africa. Their motivations can range from civil disobedience against unpopular governments, occasional drug use, or the necessity to survive in jobless poverty.

In countries with high unemployment, the black market provides workers with net wages that may exceed those of the formal economy. The tax differential between net and gross wages forms the basis of wage negotiations, with untaxed money being divided between the worker and the employer. In impoverished nations, the informal economy often represents the sole source of income for the unemployed, who typically have less bargaining power.

The black market can offer more affordable prices for local goods and services to families struggling with financial hardship. Buyers, aware of the tax savings, will often demand a share of the unpaid taxes, ensuring that the service provider does not pocket the full amount. In a buyer's market, black market prices can drop to levels equivalent to tax-exempt prices. Consequently, prices in the black market can be appreciably lower than those in the formal economy, as they are not burdened by income and sales taxes. In some EU countries, taxes can account for up to 50% of the selling price. In the US, the tax-to-GDP ratio is about 30%, but it can be higher in states with high taxes such as New York, California or Illinois.

Finally, the black market can bypass restrictions on free press and information in authoritarian regimes. Examples include the clandestine distribution of newspapers in Hong Kong, the smuggling of satellite TV tuners in Iran, or the trafficking of foreign movies on USB sticks in North Korea.

## *The black market always relies on untraceable currencies*

To circumvent regulations, the black market conceals its operations and avoids any paper trail, such as invoicing or printed contracts, thereby keeping its transactions outside the purview of the regular economy. As a result, the currencies used in these transactions must be untraceable. Often, payments are settled in banknotes outside of any bank account, with approximately 70% of black market transactions conducted in cash. Alternative currencies such as silver coins, collectible stamps, cryptocurrencies, or foreign currencies are also used.

Currency controls remain the best option to combat the black market. Severe policing to penetrate its secrecy might eradicate it, but this approach is dangerous for civil rights. Legalizing certain activities —such as controlled drug programs or low-tax products—can also create unintended consequences.

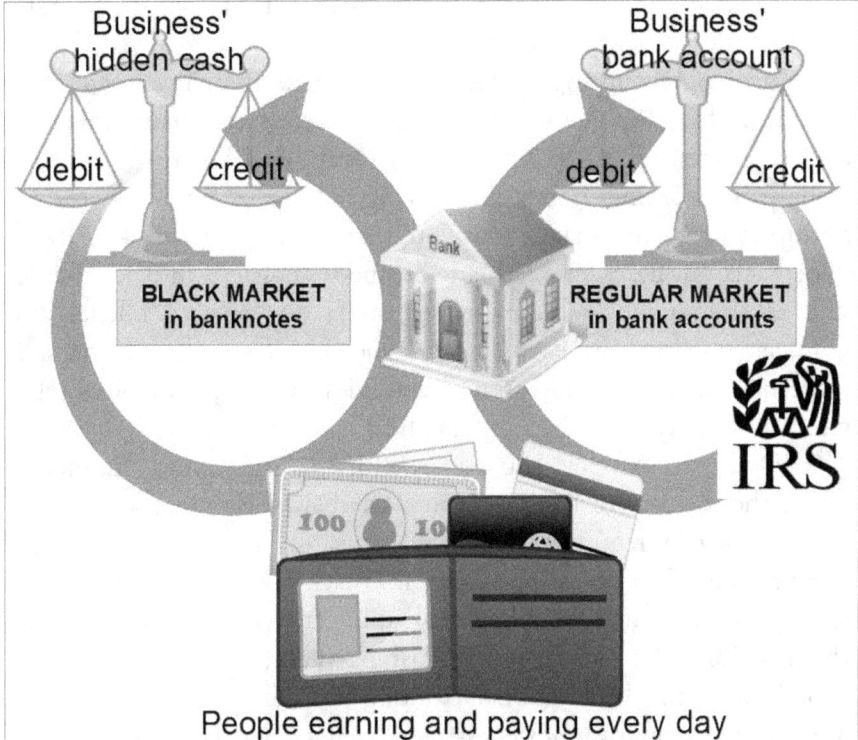

**People earning and paying every day**

*Banknotes used in underground transactions tend to keep circulating within the black economy, moving between purchases, sales, wages, and loans—all outside the bank accounts of the formal economy and recorded only in concealed ledgers. Eventually, these banknotes return to the regular economy when they are used as anonymous payments in supermarkets or gas stations.*

*The black market operates as a true parallel economy. It can, apart from the regular economy, help alleviate poverty by providing financial relief and opportunities for those who might otherwise be excluded.*

## Containing the black market of international crime

It is crucial to prevent large-scale criminals, terrorists, and fraudsters from thriving in the black market. These offenders earn millions of dollars through illegal activities such as drug smuggling or running underground sweatshops while avoiding taxes by hiding their operations or underreporting income to tax authorities.

Restraining the black market begins with identifying signs of illegal transactions and prosecuting the offenders. This effort involves not only IRS agents and the police but also participation from the banking system.

1. Invoice Accounting Inspection: A meticulous analysis of invoice accounting by IRS agents or specialized software can detect inconsistencies between tax filings and actual operations. This involves scrutinizing real working hours, identifying fake expenses, underpriced inventory, or overestimated waste, and uncovering the black market's hidden accounting practices. Many businesses engaged in black market activities maintain dual accounting books to separate official and unofficial transactions. Payments for goods and services can be split between regular and underground activities, with legal invoices justifying any activity in the event of an audit.

2. Detecting Money Laundering: Identifying money laundering during the re-entry of banknotes into the banking system is essential. Banks are legally required to identify depositors and verify the origins of their funds. This poses a challenge for black market participants who need to launder money to buy high-value items like houses or cars, which typically do not accept large cash payments.

3. Monitoring International Banking Transfers: Stopping dubious international banking transfers is vital. Foreign banks must scrutinize the origins of wire transfers or large cash deposits. Anti-money laundering laws, aimed at combating international terrorism, require collaboration between foreign nations and tax havens with industrialized countries. The Financial Action Task Force (FATF), an intergovernmental body, sets international standards for anti-money laundering and maintains a blacklist of countries to be closely monitored.

These policies aim to contain the black market as much as possible and to curtail the illicit activities that undermine legal economic and social structures.

## Estimating of the US black market at $2 trillion

The black market is estimated to constitute approximately 35% of the gross domestic product (GDP) in developing nations and about 13% of GDP in most developed countries. In the United States, the black market could be valued at over $2 to $3 trillion. Of course, these figures are rough estimates due to the inherent challenges in quantifying an illegal economy without formal reporting. Such estimates rely on identifying anomalies in economic indicators across countries to reveal the extent of black market activities. For instance, discrepancies between official production figures and reported waste, abnormally high electricity consumption in specific areas, and other indicators of hidden production can signal the presence of a black market.

*It is important to distinguish the black market from tax havens (as in the picture). Tax havens operate within legal boundaries, often maintaining bilateral tax agreements with various nations, and have the legal authority to offer reduced tax rates to foreign investors. This practice is categorized as tax optimization or tax avoidance, which is entirely separate from black market activities.*

*Tax havens may never completely disappear. Although they participate in initiatives against organized crime and terrorism, their tax advantages remain legal and persist, offering economic benefits to the havens providing services to their affluent clients.*

*Even if a standardized global tax rate were established to eliminate legal tax avoidance in these havens, it would not eradicate the black market activities of international criminals. In fact, higher taxes could increase incentives for fraud and corruption within bureaucratic societies.*

## The black market: A ceiling on taxation

Most Western democracies are reluctant to crack down on underground activities conducted by low-income unemployed individuals. These people are struggling, they do little harm, they vote, and they pay in cash without leaving concrete evidence such as bank statements. In the end, many governments do not really want to fix the inadequate oversight.

In the United States or the United Kingdom, governments often prefer to reduce tax rates and regulations to disincentivize participation in the black market. This approach aligns with other pro-business arguments for maintaining low taxes and minimal regulations.

In countries like Greece, Italy, and Belgium, the economy harbors a significant black market due to inadequate controls. As a result, the effective tax rate is considerably lower than the nominal tax rate once tax deductions and black-market activities are taken into account. In these nations, there is a degree of hypocrisy: individuals can work in the black market while receiving unemployment benefits. They may also be counted as poor in statistics despite prospering in the black market. This inflated poverty rate enables their governments to secure additional European Union funds.

In summary, the presence of a black market restrains taxation, as it incentivizes governments to lower tax rates or to accept a disparity between a low effective tax rate—which is good for the private economy—and high nominal tax rates, which may help win votes on the left of the political spectrum.

*The Most Famous Black Market: Prohibition in the 1920s, illustrated by the confiscated alcohol in the picture, remains a poignant reminder for politicians of the unintended consequences of such enforcement policies, particularly the dangerous boost to organized crime. The key lesson from this period is that laws alone cannot resolve all societal issues. The black market can only be partially contained by law enforcement, and complete eradication would require severely restricting personal freedoms.*

## High taxes without a black market: France hits a wall

France, with its heavy taxes and rigid controls, is one of the few countries that has successfully suppressed the black market for small-scale activities in sectors such as housing and retail. However, this success has not extended to addressing black market activities linked to burglaries, high-level criminality, and terrorism. Moreover, stringent enforcement has left young unemployed individuals struggling to find customers for handyman services in the black market, pushing many towards drug trafficking, which bypasses the need for receipts.

To prevent hidden transactions, France supports one of the most intrusive tax administrations in the world, meticulously inspecting every invoice of every tax return to limit the black market. This extensive surveillance is costly, not only in terms of wages for civil servants but also in the paperwork burden it imposes on the French population.

These stringent controls allow France to maintain a high tax-to-GDP ratio of about 45%—one of the highest in the world—without being undermined by black-market activity. France can then impose high taxes, which are often passed on to consumers through higher selling prices. This system places a disproportionately heavy burden on the purchases of the poor compared with those of the rich.

Despite high taxes and minimal black market activity, France has not resolved its economic and social challenges. The country does not outperform others in the number of technology startups or in reducing unemployment rates. On the contrary, its suburbs frequently erupt in riots as unemployed residents, often with migrant backgrounds, feel excluded. Rural areas express discontent through movements like the "yellow jackets" (gilets jaunes), showing support for the far right and rejecting an establishment perceived as wasting public funds.

France intends to lower its tax rates, but efforts to reform its high-tax system are often thwarted by demonstrations from civil servants. This resistance to budget cuts delays any meaningful tax reform, which cannot proceed without addressing public expenditures, given the country's considerable public debt.

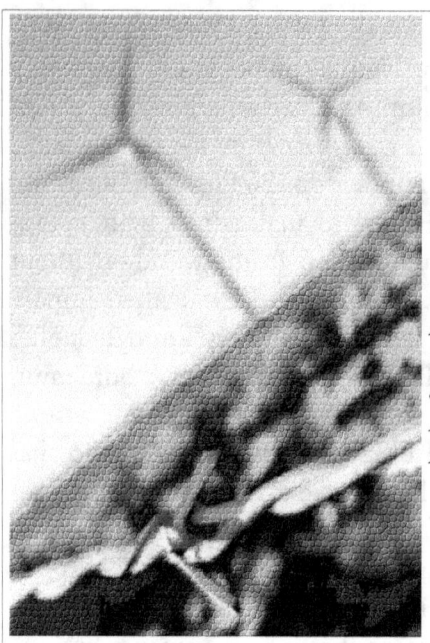

The crackdown by some governments on their small-scale black markets is excessive. These pettifogging controls primarily benefit the government and its civil servants, while imposing unjust burdens on family shops and small businesses already struggling with stagnant wages for decades.

An example of this overreach would be the punishment of an underground business producing and selling green energy at net cost, which would contribute to preventing global warming (as illustrated in the picture). The bureaucratic government prefers its complex system of taxes, subsidies (which do not always offset the taxes included in the selling price), permits for wind turbines, and carbon pricing measures, all of which stifle small businesses.

Based on these considerations, understanding the black market is a springboard towards the next chapter.

## Historical Correlation: Economists Overlook Parallel Economies and Their Potential to Reduce Inequalities

Economists often overlook the black market and parallel currencies in their research, treating these topics as curiosities rather than subjects of serious study. However, it is important to recognize the potential spillover effects of an overly regulated economy into the black market.

In the US, this underestimation can be attributed to the perception that the black market is relatively small. Additionally, economists often work in academic environments, removed from the on-the-ground realities where underground or parallel economies are more visible.

In Europe, countries with meaningful black markets rarely acknowledge their extent. Governments tend to understate the prevalence of the black market for two reasons: to give their citizens some leeway and to exclude underground economic activity from official GDP calculations. The latter is crucial, as official GDP figures are used by European institutions to determine EU contributions and subsidies. Some countries, like Greece and Belgium, are notoriously permissive about their black markets while benefiting from European subsidies based on their lower official GDP.

Despite the under-reporting of the black market and parallel currencies, these areas warrant serious study. Could the establishment of a parallel economy, complete with its own currency, benefit society?

# CHAPTER 4:

# A NEW CURRENCY FOR

# A PARALLEL ECONOMY

(An alternative market
to reduce inequalities and
fight global warming)

Inequality and global warming are the two armies launching a pincer movement on a society polarized about the strategy.

In the context of persistent inequality, low-income workers are rejecting the establishment and its green agenda, demanding a focus on domestic job creation and wage increases.

Concerning global warming, the younger generation is challenging free-market capitalism that relies on cheap energy, leaning towards progressive and even socialist ideologies.

As a prerequisite for this chapter, the book "Fighting Global Warming: Problematic economic implications" cautions against demagogic solutions. It argues that government intervention has limited impact; real progress depends on new technologies and the private sector to create jobs, including green jobs. To date, the government has not found a way to accelerate this growth effectively. There is no "magic mix" of regulations and taxation that can resolve these issues of low wages and global warming, leaving the government unable to take decisive action beyond implementing symbolic minimum wages and engaging in superficial greenwashing.

## A Tax-Free Parallel Market for Higher Wages

*A new tax-free market outside of the regular and black markets*

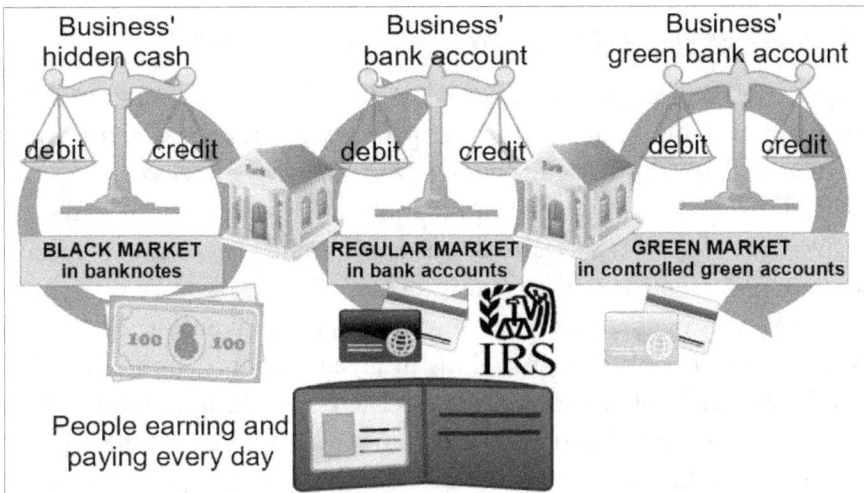

The next pages, based on the drawing above, will examine the feasibility of establishing a new market outside the regular economy and away from the black market.

The preliminary condition is to isolate this new market from the existing markets. It hinges on confining the new market within its own accounting framework.

The final steps will aim to attract individuals, investors, businesses, and perhaps workers displaced by AI to this new market, and to encourage Congress to adopt it.

Could a new tax-exempt market, operating legally yet functioning somewhat like the black market, be established? This market would operate independently from the conventional taxed economy while remaining distinct from the illicit black market. In other words, it would require separate accounting systems, distinct from both the regular economy and the black market.

To encourage participation, this framework would eliminate all forms of taxation—including income, corporate, sales, and potentially payroll taxes. At the same time, like the black market, it should generate investment returns and well-paying jobs. Motivation among participants is key: people need strong incentives to take part, and profits or wages are essential for any thriving economy.

This new parallel market could aptly be referred to as the *"green-*

*market*," alluding to its black-market counterpart while highlighting its "green" content. Unlike the black market, however, this system should serve the broader interests of society. All its components—including products, corporations, workers, and banks—would be labeled as "*green.*"

## A green-currency held exclusively in green-accounts

To isolate the green-market, a distinct digital currency, supported by banking controls, could ensure the market's full segregation from the regular dollars. This currency would exist exclusively in electronic form within bank accounts, with no option for withdrawal in physical banknotes. Such a specialized currency could be termed "green-currency," "green-money," or "green-dollar."

Implementing such a digital-only currency would enable the precise supervision of banking transactions in green-accounts, similar to how banks currently filter out terrorism-related and illicit activities. This digital control would protect the tax-exempt green economy, which is dedicated exclusively to the production and trade of green-products and green-services, avoiding polluting regular products and prohibited drugs. The tax-exempt status is granted in exchange for stringent controls.

The green-money accounts should not overwhelm banks and payment processing companies, as they already manage foreign currencies. Many banks are experienced in handling deposits and loans in both dollars and euros for their corporate clients. Their existing banking software would only require minor adjustments, such as adding a new green-dollar sign alongside the traditional dollar sign ($) and the euro sign (€).

This form of tax shielding through currency would be simpler than bureaucratic controls involving subsidies or tax breaks. A tax-free parallel market with its own currency could easily accommodate existing companies that cannot always operate under complex tax rules or within the confines of a tax-free restricted zone near a remote coastal harbor.

*Criminal activities are likely to continue using gold coins or physical banknotes, as illustrated in the image, to evade the banking oversight imposed by authorities on dollar transactions.*

*Remarkably, such illicit cash flows CANNOT mingle with a secondary, voluntary, tax-free green-currency that is fully recorded in bank accounts. Criminals will avoid the green-market and its banking controls. Instead, they will remain in their black market, using exclusively gold coins or paper banknotes of the regular currency. This avoidance principle serves as the cornerstone of the green-market: establishing a parallel digital-only currency COULD separate the accounting of the new green economy from both the regular and black markets.*

## Creation of green-dollars by the banking system

To initiate the creation of green-dollars, Congress would authorize a conversion mechanism between regular dollars and green-dollars at the Federal Reserve, with both currencies pegged at par for exchange purposes. This exchange would be akin to the historical conversion of dollar bills into gold coins. In this way, the total money supply—the sum of ordinary dollars and green-dollars—would not initially change.

Banking institutions would then be able to convert regular dollars into green-dollars at the Fed. Under supervision, they could also exchange ordinary dollars for green-dollars among themselves on the foreign exchange market, notifying the Fed but without going directly through its facilities.

Banks would then offer deposit and credit accounts denominated in green-dollars. Companies engaged in green activities, as well as individuals, could receive loans denominated in this currency.

## Control of the green-accounts of voluntary green-corporations

Authorized green-corporations would open green deposit and credit accounts. They would conduct all transactions exclusively through these green-accounts using the green-currency, ensuring a self-contained system. Green-corporations would pay green-dollars to a provider's regular dollar account to purchase from the regular economy; the payment system would automatically convert these funds into the currency of the receiving accounts. In the opposite direction, green-corporations could receive regular dollars immediately converted into green-dollars as payment for the sale of green-products. In this manner, the two markets could interact and trade much like neighboring countries, with currency exchanges at the border.

These green-accounts would always be subject to rigorous audits to verify that tax-exempt payments and income are directly tied to the production of approved green-products. Green-banks would scrutinize these transactions before authorizing the conversion and transfer of green-dollars into regular dollar accounts. Oversight of green-accounts would detect irregularities such as unusual gas consumption or unjustified tax-exempt labor. Regulatory auditors could compare corporate metrics related to raw materials, supplier inputs, and workforce levels against average ratios observed in the green-accounts of industry peers.

Green-corporations can benefit from tax-exempt status, but this privilege must be subject to strict oversight to ensure transparency and adherence to the system's guidelines. Only voluntary green-corporations would have their green-accounts subject to supplementary audits, ensuring transparency and compliance within the green-market. Such robust regulatory systems already exist for other corporations going public in the stock market, requiring frequent auditing by firms such as Deloitte or KPMG.

## No control for green-wage earners

Green-wages would be exempt from direct controls, as the green-money paid by employers would already have undergone clearance procedures at the corporate level. Green-workers would accept green-wages if the compensation is favorable compared with net wages in the regular economy. Their earnings would be credited to their green-accounts.

Green-workers could spend their wages on green-products or exchange their green-dollars for regular dollars at their bank whenever they wish. For holders of green-accounts, transactions involving the exchange of green-dollars and regular dollars would resemble credit-card payments in foreign currencies, with only a single transaction line appearing in their respective bank statements.

Alternatively, green-workers could choose to save their earnings in green-accounts, allowing banks to invest these funds within the green market. They could also invest their green-dollars in green-corporations, keeping capital circulating within the system. The same approach would apply to shareholders of green-corporations, who could reinvest their tax-free dividends, further supporting growth and sustainability within the green-economy.

Regular households could as well legally earn tax-free green-dollars through side jobs within the green-market. For instance, they could install solar panels on their residential roofs and sell the electricity to a green-electricity distributor, with controls applied seamlessly through the green-corporation's green-account. Their extra tax-free income in green-currency could be spent on other green-products, invested in green-corporations, or simply exchanged for regular dollars. This concept is similar in structure to the black market, where individuals participate informally for a few hours a week outside their primary employment—though here it would occur within a fully legal framework.

## The rest of the economy unaffected

The stringent oversight within the green-market would not affect the regular producers and consumers of conventional taxable goods paid in regular currency, as only the voluntary green-corporations within the green-market would be subject to close regulatory scrutiny.

Any criminal or underground transactions will continue to use regular dollar banknotes. Such activities must avoid the voluntary green-currency, which is fully traceable by auditors due to its digital nature and mandatory recording in bank accounts.

Meanwhile, the IRS would continue to tax traditional incomes in regular currency, while maintaining its vigilance in identifying illicit transactions within conventional bank accounts.

## Tax-free green-products

The affordability of green products should increase due to their lower tax-free prices, which would expand the range of buyers. Economies of scale should then drive prices down even further, enabling more consumers to purchase an increasing number of green products.

Potential green-products and green-services could include:
• power plants with solar panels or wind turbines;
• solar panels installation on residential rooftops;
• timber for housing, aimed at $CO_2$ sequestration;
• battery packs;
• heat pump manufacturing and installation;
• carbon removal products;
• nuclear power plants for electricity providers;
• components for all green-products listed above, potentially supplied by new green subsidiaries of existing corporations.

YOU'RE NEXT!

⟨*Louisville Herald*⟩

*Will prices of green products decrease if taxes are eliminated? Yes, they should, driven by competitive dynamics among providers striving to increase their market share by offering lower prices.*

*This economic competition will, of course, require a vigilant consumer base ready to take legal action against corporations engaging in price fixing or violating antitrust laws, reminiscent of the 1907 Roosevelt vs. Paper Trust case. Equally crucial is the role of a free and investigative press capable of exposing unethical activities, whether perpetrated by greedy CEOs or corrupt politicians. Most importantly, the best safeguard against inflated prices is a vibrant startup ecosystem ready to challenge larger corporations with competitive pricing. Individual responsibility remains an indispensable factor, as in any democratic society that champions free markets.*

## *Tax-free green products: Prices possibly down 50%*

A myriad of taxes end up in the final price of all product categories, including green products. This means that consumers of clean energy and green alternatives pay for the sales tax (direct taxation), but they also pay for prices that must incorporate custom tolls, income taxes on the workers building the wind turbines or solar panels, income taxes of part suppliers, permit fees for installation, and more (indirect taxation). All taxes and fees invariably contribute to the final prices paid by consumers. This overall taxation on all products is higher than generally perceived.

On average, taxes in the US account for approximately 28% of GDP, based on the tax-to-GDP ratio, which includes federal, state, county, and municipal taxes but excludes Social Security taxes, as they are not factored into GDP calculations. In some European countries, this tax burden can reach up to 45% of GDP, according to international tax-to-GDP measurements.

Since household consumption makes up about 70% of US GDP, the tax-to-GDP ratio provides insight into the portion of selling prices that reflects taxation. However, the actual tax component in selling prices varies. It can be close to zero for free public services like roads, relatively low for subsidized goods and services, or significantly higher for products and services with high labor costs. For instance, in the US, consumption products that rely heavily on highly paid engineers may have an effective tax burden of up to 50%, while in the EU, this could reach 60%. The taxes collected from these higher-cost goods ultimately help fund essential public services such as infrastructure and education.

Taxes are not always paid by the rich to benefit the poor; in many cases, the distribution of tax burdens and benefits is more intricate. Any form of taxation can potentially affect the poor more than the rich. For example, sales taxes disproportionately burden low-income individuals because they consume a higher share of their income, whereas higher-income individuals spend a smaller proportion. This regressive nature of sales taxes is widely acknowledged by economists, which is why most US states exempt groceries from them.

Income tax presents a more complex scenario. Raising the tax rates of the highest tax brackets may target high-wage earners and corporations, but the indirect tax burden (or "**tax incidence**") can shift to consumers. If individual or corporate suppliers pass on the cost of income taxes through higher prices, both low- and high-income individuals bear part of the burden.

The black market reinforces the observation that the income tax burden falls on consumers as well as suppliers. Black-market consumers and providers typically negotiate to share the tax savings compared to the selling price in the formal economy, which includes all forms of taxation. These savings include any income or corporate taxes that are omitted from black-market invoices. As a result, black-market consumers benefit from lower costs due to the absence of income taxation, whereas in the formal economy the same purchase would place the full tax liability of the regular market price on the buyer. This illustrates that the incidence of income tax is shared between consumers and providers, rather than falling solely on corporate or individual providers.

Such a dynamic should encourage a thoughtful examination of how a tax-free parallel economy, akin to the black market, could help reduce costs for low-income consumers.

## Green-jobs and higher wages

Lower prices would attract more buyers in the tax-free green-market. This growth would encourage greater corporate participation, creating more job opportunities for all workers, including those with lower incomes. Employers may need to offer competitive wages—either as net wages in the green-market or as gross wages in the regular economy that yield an equivalent take-home pay.

The increase in net wages would not come directly from tax savings on green wages, as only selling prices would reflect those savings. Instead, wage growth would be driven by overall market expansion, with employers competing for workers by offering higher net wages in the green market or higher gross wages in the traditional economy.

*Other regulations and taxation policies should be implemented with caution. As discussed in "Inequality and Economic Policies: Just tax the rich?," governments have tried numerous subsidy programs over recent decades, but many have underperformed due to excessive complexity and poor follow-up after implementation.*

*Given this, the green-market presents a viable alternative with the potential to stimulate job growth and increase wages. Moreover, further benefits could help reduce inequality and address global warming, as explored in the following pages.*

## No more complex than the regular economy

The green-market system would not be more complicated than today's economy. It would simply be another financial tool to manage, much like tracking work hours or managing standard accounting tasks. This system would be neither more complex than a bank account.

Workers and businesses would quickly adapt to this new configuration of green-bank accounts, as it allows them to earn income. The primary appeal is financial gain, not environmental activism. The green-market will succeed if people can manage their finances and bank accounts independently, without excessive government oversight or bureaucratic interference.

## Tax-free: Minimal impact on the Treasury

The development of the green-market should not be hindered by concerns over potential tax revenue losses. First, any perceived shortfall could be offset by economic gains from job creation and higher wages within this new market, which would reduce reliance on welfare programs. Second, green products are currently relatively scarce, and a significant tax shortfall is unlikely given that the small number of corporations that have transitioned to green energy represents only a minor share of the IRS's tax base.

The green-market could also replace existing subsidy programs, which are being phased out as they lose political support due to their inefficiencies and limitations:

1: Cost to the government: Subsidies can strain the treasury if they exceed the difference between tax revenues included in the prices of green-products and those associated with goods powered by gasoline or natural gas. Caution: green subsidies are not generously offered by governments, as they rarely offset the numerous taxes included in the prices of green-products; and, when they do, governments are merely returning what they have collected elsewhere.

2: Bureaucratic complexity: The intricate subsidy application and approval process can be overwhelming, often discouraging small businesses and households from applying.

3: Favoring the wealthy: Amortizing the cost of solar panels requires a long-term commitment to recover the investment, even with subsidies. This can discourage struggling businesses and individuals, unlike wealthier households with a more secure financial future.

4: Arbitrary amounts loosely linked to carbon reductions: Subsidies do not always result in a lower carbon footprint.

5: Politicized or "picking market winners and losers": Governments may design subsidy programs that favor products manufactured in politically favorable precincts.

6: "Market distortion": Subsidies that guarantee a fixed purchasing price for green electricity over a 10-year period may unintentionally discourage energy producers from investing in cost-reduction improvements. This can create market price distortions, where subsidized prices remain higher than those in a competitive, unsubsidized market. However, this observation is less relevant for one-time subsidies for residential solar panel installations, where numerous service providers compete for swift project execution.

In response to these criticisms, subsidies are being reduced year after year, especially as renewable power plants and electric vehicles are becoming competitive without government support. Governments are even considering eliminating all subsidies and replacing them with a carbon tax to discourage the use of fossil fuels and continue to accelerate the green transition.

*With subsidies likely to be phased out and no other clear method to untax clean energy, governments are left with energy-efficiency standards and carbon taxation schemes designed to reduce emissions in a market-friendly way. However, stringent regulations and carbon pricing mechanisms, such as the EU Emissions Trading System, have produced limited results in lowering emissions while also placing a disproportionate burden on low-income households. These policies have had minimal impact on job creation and carbon reduction and should be reconsidered.*

*A key issue with strict energy standards and carbon taxation is that low-income households allocate three times more of their budget to energy costs compared to higher-income households (source: US Department of Energy). Additionally, industries such as mining face the risk of job losses. While some subsidies attempt to offset these costs, they are often inaccessible to those who exceed income thresholds. As a result, low-income workers bear the greatest burden of carbon regulations, leading many to support politicians who oppose such measures. This resistance has made it difficult to sustain energy regulations, and any proposed carbon taxation bill is widely viewed as politically unviable in the US Congress.*

*A tax-free parallel system could offer a solution by shifting the focus from penalties to incentives. Instead of imposing energy regulations and carbon taxes, this approach would create jobs and encourage tax-free production.*

## A New Gray-Money to Supervise
## the Green-Market

### *A new gray-money within green-accounts*

The price in green-money should not be viewed as a gauge of carbon consumption from fossil energy in the manufacturing of end products. Instead, the primary purpose of green-money is to provide a tax-exempt advantage, encouraging the consumption of environmentally friendly green-products. That said, the development of a carbon footprint indicator is still feasible and could be integrated within the green-accounts.

A gray-dollar could strengthen the system as a carbon gauge. This complementary unit would be symbolized by the color gray, evoking crude oil or anthracite coal. The color-coding feature would integrate with green-banking software. Bank engineers would create two separate transaction databases: one for green-currency and one for gray-currency. As with traditional currencies, these units would never mix and could only be exchanged for one another in currency markets. The green-money and gray-money systems would leave the regular dollar-based banking software untouched. They would largely mirror existing banking infrastructure, with one key modification: the introduction of new symbols to replace the familiar "$."

It would be strongly recommended that banks merge both accounts into a single, user-friendly interface. This integration would simplify the customers' management of the new dual-currency green-accounts. In this context, green-accounts would imply handling both green- and gray-currencies.

### *Introduction of gray-cents*

Initially, gray-money, like green-money, would be exchanged for regular dollars at Federal Reserve counters. Subsequently, a symbolic tax of a few gray-cents could replace a portion of the existing federal excise taxes on each sale of a gallon of gas or a few pounds of coal. This distinctly visible carbon tax in gray-cents would equate one gallon of gas with 8.5 pounds of coal, as one gallon of gasoline emits approximately the same amount of $CO_2$ as 8.5 pounds of coal, according to the EPA. The same principle would apply to other greenhouse gas sources, such as gallons of butane, gallons of liquid hydrogen derived from natural gas, or megawatt-hours of electricity from coal power plants.

In response to this new symbolic carbon tax in gray-money, petroleum and coal producers would implement gray-money accounting alongside their standard financial reporting. This adaptation would enable them to start billing each unit of gas or coal in both currencies. Similar to operations in the regular and black markets, billing in two currencies should not disrupt corporations, as they are often capable of managing dual accounting systems.

Coal and oil industries would include the gray-cents collected within the federal excise tax payments to the IRS for each gallon of gas or pound of coal sold. The IRS would then be authorized to exchange its gray-money for regular dollars at the Federal Reserve, thereby restoring the income from the excise tax in regular dollars. This system would indirectly provide precise measurements of domestic $CO_2$ emissions from fossil fuels on a monthly basis.

## *Tracking fossil fuel consumption with gray-cents for voluntary corporations*

Corporations committed to achieving carbon neutrality may choose to integrate gray-cents into their pricing. These corporations could market their carbon-neutral processes, potentially increasing their market share. This decision might be driven by growing consumer demand for transparency, with clear gray-cent pricing labels on store products.

These participating corporations would open a green-account to manage the gray-currency and ensure that gray-cents cannot be converted into regular dollars. Purchases made partially in gray-cents could only be offset by sales that also include gray-cents, with no way around this due to the nonexistence of physical gray-money banknotes. Alternatively, gray-cents could be managed through loans that must eventually be repaid via sales in gray-cents. Corporations would then adhere to the gray-cents system to account for, label, and sell their products at a hybrid price—combining both standard dollars and gray-cents—thereby enabling the tracking of the coal and gas consumption embedded in their products.

Reluctant downstream corporate consumers of petroleum and coal would have the right to ignore their carbon footprint. The accounting of gray-cents would be voluntary. These non-participating corporations would simply pay all excise taxes on fossil fuels, with their credit cards automatically handling any necessary currency exchange for gray-cents, as is currently done for international payments. Of course, these corporations could always change their minds if their consumers explicitly demanded the option to pay in gray-cents.

### *Easier control of green-corporations: Gray-cents fit perfectly with green-money*

The use of gray-cents for regulatory control would be mandatory for green-corporations that have voluntarily entered the green-market. It is crucial to remember that the green-market is tax-free in exchange for strict auditing. Green-corporations are not authorized to resell non-compliant products tax-free.

Regulatory oversight is automated through the banking system, ensuring that the input of fossil fuels is accurately accounted for in the labeling of all output sales. Matching in-and-out flows between bank accounts would suffice, making this process less cumbersome than a bureaucratic eco-friendly regulatory code.

High prices in gray-cents or the accumulation of debts in gray-cents would expose unscrupulous green-corporations or their suppliers with high fossil fuel usage. The worst polluters among green-corporations could face gray-cent insolvency as authorities expel them from the green-market, or as consumers shift their preferences toward cleaner green-products.

Unlike untraceable black-market transactions, carbon cheating by green-corporations would be difficult to conceal. In this sense, gray-cents are a perfect complement to green-money, ensuring transparency and accountability.

## *Gray-cents for individuals: Eye-opening*

At the end of the consumption chain, individuals and households would have the option to pay with gray-cents, following any necessary currency exchange. If they choose to disregard the green-market, any purchase in gray-cents would be automatically converted into dollar-cents by their credit card provider or by the cashier if paying with dollar bills.

Those opening a green account that handles both gray and green currencies could estimate the carbon footprint associated with their total gray-cent spending, which reflects their direct or indirect consumption of fossil fuels. These individuals could even obtain an accurate carbon footprint provided they purchase exclusively from corporations participating in the gray-cent system. Such gray-money amounts would serve as a highly precise tracker of fossil fuel emissions for each consumer.

To streamline transactions, participants could use a smartphone payment app or a dual-currency credit card. These payment tools would draw upon regular dollars from the conventional account and gray-cents from the green-account. The payment app or credit card software could even estimate $CO_2$ emissions linked to transactions from non-participating corporations, using a symbolic conversion to gray-cents—potentially overestimated to ensure climate safety—providing a view of the carbon footprint.

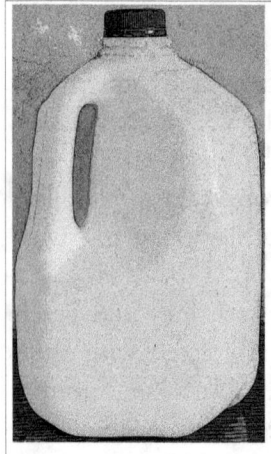

There is about half a pound of $CO_2$ emissions per dollar of US GDP according to the World Bank, while burning a gallon of gasoline releases about 20 pounds of $CO_2$ emissions. Derived from these figures, a rough estimate suggests that around 40 dollars of GDP is generated per gallon of gasoline.

Therefore, if 40 gray-cents are taxed on each gallon of gasoline, there would be about 1 gray-cent per dollar of output made from scratch in the US. According to this number, a gallon of milk (picture) could be priced at $4 and 5 gray-cents, but another brand could be priced at $5 and only 4 gray-cents.

This scenario poses an intriguing question: which bottle would the eco-friendly customer choose? Is it possible that they would opt for the product with the smallest carbon footprint? The answer can only be determined through a tax-free green-money system, where both green-dollars and gray-cents work together for accurate traceability. This represents another key idea underpinning the system. Testing the system in a limited area will reveal its effectiveness. If it fails, the gray-cent tax can simply be reverted to regular cents in the excise tax.

## Ratcheting up the tax in gray-cents? Maybe never

If the consumption of petroleum and coal products does not decrease rapidly enough, despite the establishment of a competitive green-market, it may become necessary to impose additional carbon penalties in full gray-dollars on these items to mitigate the impacts of global warming.

Any form of carbon pricing must be considered a last resort, as it may face resistance from the middle class. Hopefully, such drastic measures will not be necessary. Moreover, an alternative strategy could guide the green economy toward net-zero emissions: the implementation of gray-cent quotas.

## Make the Rich Pay More

### Quotas of gray-cents

The gray-cent concept could pave the way for implementing carbon quotas for individuals. Under this paradigm, a reasonable quota of gray-cents could be granted at no charge to each individual or household, but not to corporations. This quota could be determined from the data collected during the prior phase of voluntary gray-cent usage.

A quota of gray-cents would offer a significant advantage over carbon pricing: individuals could avoid penalties as long as they remain within their allotted quota. This approach would be more manageable for low-income households than for the wealthy, whose lifestyles often involve larger properties, private jets, and luxury yachts.

Gee! But I Feel Satisfied With Life!

*Recent economic studies show that the top 10% of Americans account for 50% of all consumer spending, contributing to roughly 40% of greenhouse gas emissions. This raises an important question: Should this group continue to have the unchecked right to emit such a large share of pollution?*

*There is a strong case for requiring them to offset their disproportionate environmental impact. One approach could involve reducing their household energy use through measures like installing solar panels and battery storage systems. However, these efforts have limited impact when it comes to more carbon-intensive activities, such as private air travel. In such instances, financial compensation or other forms of carbon offset may be necessary to more fully address their environmental footprint.*

## Quotas on consumption items and long-term assets

The quantification of consumption items like staple foods, electricity, or gasoline purchases can be readily accounted for in the monthly quota according to their cost in gray-cents.

For durable goods such as cars, housing, or sailboats, which have long-term consumption patterns, an equitable framework could address both new and existing assets that were not subject to gray-cent charges at the time of their purchase. Several compensation options could be considered:

• New constructions: These might be required to secure a loan in gray-cents to account for their construction carbon footprint.

• Existing assets: A simplified mechanism could apply, such as a retrospective construction tax based on criteria like the square footage of a home or the asset's cost relative to the GDP dollar per carbon output for past purchases.

• Daily or monthly cost: Potential buyers or renters should consider energy efficiency, such as insulation quality and expected utility costs, when evaluating a property.

• Exemptions: Exemptions could be granted for smaller assets, including compact houses (e.g., 1,000 square feet for two people), smaller vehicles, or electric vehicles, recognizing their lower impact.

This approach aims to balance carbon footprint accountability across different asset classes while considering the historical context of their construction and usage.

## Monitoring cash withdrawals from regular accounts

All participants in the gray-cent quota system would be required to use the designated gray-cent payment application. This system would need to monitor cash withdrawals from standard bank accounts to ensure that anonymous banknotes are not used for unauthorized fossil fuel purchases, such as filling a gas tank.

To enforce this, mobile payment applications could incorporate features to record purchases made with cash and even track GPS data related to vehicle or private jet usage to detect discrepancies in gray-cent consumption. Alternatively, a fuel-tracking device could be required for gas-powered vehicles, while electric vehicles would be exempt. Other monitoring solutions could also be considered. Tracking should be relatively straightforward, as gasoline is the only fuel that can be purchased with cash.

Cash transactions in bars, restaurants, and other small-scale purchases would not impact the quota system significantly due to their low volume of gray-cents. Businesses might also choose to reject cash payments if they need to account for and pass on their own gray-cent costs to consumers.

One last possible measure could be to limit participants in the gray-cent system to savings accounts only, eliminating access to regular checking accounts. A linked green account could then be required to pull transaction data from existing checking accounts, enabling cross-checking and monitoring of any unaccounted fossil fuel consumption.

## *Corporations: Just passing it on to consumers*

Corporations would be unaffected by individual gray-cent quotas, as these quotas would only apply to consumers. This approach contrasts with carbon credit quotas under schemes like the EU ETS or WCI, which are applied to the production side, and whose costs from exceeding quotas are often discreetly passed on to consumers through higher prices.

Implementing this system of gray-cent quotas for individuals would require every corporation to trace gray-cents through mandatory green-accounts and incorporate their gray-cent costs as a distinct supplement to the selling price in regular dollars of every output.

Individuals, regardless of their wealth, would be unable to evade their quota allowances for hidden purchases, as they would have no way to obtain gray-cents under the counter and deposit them into their closely supervised gray-cent accounts. Regular bank accounts could also be accessed for quota controls. Participation in the green-market system would remain voluntary for most individuals, but it might involve multiple layers of oversight.

## *A market for unused quotas: make the rich pay*

Only the wealthiest segment of the population would initially be pressured to enter the green-market system with green-accounts and gray-cent quotas. Initially, this group could be limited to regular users of private jets or luxury yachts powered by fossil fuels. Over time, regulations could expand to encompass 10% or more of the population with stricter quotas.

Affluent individuals would face fines in full dollars for their excessive carbon emissions, as measured by gray-cents exceeding their individual quotas. These fines could increase exponentially as the wealthy monopolize large quantities of scarce commodities or clean energy, ensuring compensation for others facing higher costs of limited resources. Importantly, such penalties on the wealthiest would impact their spending rather than their investments.

The administration collecting these penalties would allocate the funds to green projects or subsidies. Alternatively, the administration could use the money from these penalties to purchase unused individual quotas, resulting in full dollars credited for each leftover gray-cent transferred to the administration.

Instead of paying fines to an administration, individuals could trade unused quota allowances in a novel market between frugal households and high-consumption consumers. Affluent consumers could purchase unused gray-cent quotas from more restrained households using standard currency, paying a few dollars for each gray-cent. They could then spend these additional gray-cents to consume resources—such as private jet fuel—that exceed their initial gray-cent allowances.

## *Incentivizing participation: A $1,000 monthly bonus*

Quotas could provide households with several hundred dollars per week, depending on income levels. If higher-income participants actively engage in the system, the combination of tax-free green-money, green-jobs, and sales of unused gray-cent quotas could generate substantial financial benefits. For low-income households, this could translate into monthly bonuses reaching several hundred dollars—or even exceeding $1,000—enhancing economic participation and financial stability.

Low-income households could be incentivized to join the green-market, conserve more energy, and invest in energy-efficient products to maximize proceeds from their unused quota allowances in their green-accounts.

Corporations, influenced by customer demand, may also join the green market, adopting its specific accounting system and pricing their products in gray-cents. To reduce their gray-cent pricing, corporations could improve product design, cost structures, and pricing strategies for gray-cent components. Ultimately, sufficient pressure for cheaper green products could delay the need to mandate participation in the green market for both corporations and individuals.

The green transition cannot be solely the responsibility of top earners and corporations funding the shift for wasteful consumers. Nor can it rely exclusively on carbon pricing for large emitters while continuously excusing individual emissions or discouraging small businesses from growing to avoid being classified as large emitters, which negatively impacts employment. The green market must involve individual responsibility to conserve energy and create jobs for all, ensuring a balanced and sustainable transition.

## Historical Correlation: A Monetary Solution to Reduce Inequalities and Contain Global Warming?

If readers understand that the monetary system is a flexible tool with historical impact, are open to the idea of a secondary currency, recognize the existence of parallel markets like the black market, and believe that addressing inequality and global warming requires a shift away from ineffective government regulations, they may see value in the Green-Market System.

If they find no major flaws in the concept, they might consider sharing it with others—or exploring the full version of *The History of Money for Understanding Economics*, which details the evolution of monetary systems and various parallel experiments.

# Bibliography

The complete bibliography can be found in:
Lannoye, Vincent. The History of Money for Understanding Economics. 2015

# Origin of the Illustrations

| [4] www.loc.gov | [13] public domain |
| [7] Author's collection, which includes many copies | [19] Based on a picture from Thayne Tuason, via Wikimedia Commons |